multimedia graphics

multi|media Graphics

The Best of Global Hyperdesign

Edited by Willem Velthoven and Jorinde Seijdel

Preface by Neville Brody

CHRONICLE BOOKS

SAN FRANCISCO

Copyright © 1996 BIS Publishers, Amsterdam

First published in the United States in 1996 by Chronicle Books

First published in The Netherlands, Belgium, Luxemburg and Japan in 1996 by BIS Publishers

First Published in Germany, Austria and Switzerland in 1996 by Verlag Hermann Schmidt Mainz

First published in all other parts of the world in 1996 by Thames and Hudson

All Rights Reserved. No part of this book may be reproduced in any form without written permission from the publisher.

Printed and bound in Singapore by CS Graphics

Library of Congress Cataloging-in-Publication Data available.

ISBN 0-8118-1404-1

Distributed in Canada by
Raincoast Books
8680 Cambie Street
Vancouver, B.C. V6P 6M9

10 9 8 7 6 5 4 3 2 1

Chronicle Books
275 Fifth Street
San Francisco, CA 94103

Contents

Preface

The most exciting thing about multimedia and electronic publishing is the potential they hold: the potential to establish themselves as a completely new media form in their own right, the potential for a new kind of creative channel that allows us to search and uncover the undercurrent of society and learn more about ourselves through a process of revealing, not concealing. All great painting and sculpture have been effective as mirrors — reflections of our fears and hopes, our internal struggles and our social obsessions and rules. Multimedia can play that role. They are the media that best match our current obsessions and communications systems and therefore hold the greatest possibility as a transport mechanism for change and comment.

The main drawback in all of this is the lack of adventure and risk being taken in addressing a new form and in developing that form as a new language that reflects a change in human behaviour. When we 'use' an electronic publication, our very activity is altered. When the television was invented, it was designed to appear as a radio with a picture, because that

AS YOU ZOOM IN CLOSER, THE PAGES FROM FONTNET BECOME MICROCOSMS, OR WORLDS WITHIN WORLDS. THIS SYSTEM IS UTILISED BY THE MAPS WHICH DISPLAY THE INTERRELATIONSHIP OF THE VARIOUS PARTS AS MOLECULAR OR GALACTIC STRUCTURES. THE PURPOSE OF THE SITE IS TO INITIATE A WORLD–WIDE TYPOGRAPHIC FOCUS WHICH WILL COVER AREAS OF TYPE FROM FUSE EXPERIMENTATION TO FULL ALPHABET DISPLAYS.

willingness to create new forms and modes of thought for a revolutionary new form of media that needs addressing in a radically new way. The events of the next two years will be critical — it is during this period that both the textual and visual rules of the media will be established. This book presents some of those pointing the way, catalysts for the new vision necessary to break down our resistance and fears.

NEVILLE BRODY

FONTNET WENT ON–LINE IN OCTOBER 1995. IT IS OWNED AND RUN BY nWORKS LTD, LONDON. DAVE BARR AT nWORKS SET IT UP AND PROGRAMMED IT. © RESEARCH ARTS, LONDON

to the contemporary power base. In recent years, a similar view has been taken of the widespread distribution of the computer —

↓

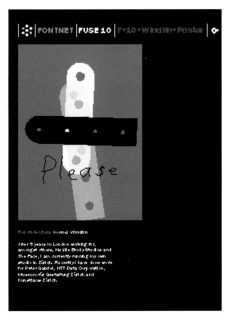

THE FONTNET SITE IS BEING SET UP AS A CENTRAL SOUR-
CE FOR TYPOGRAPHIC COMMUNICATION. RESEARCH ARTS
SEES THE SITE AS A SOLAR SYSTEM, WITH EACH PART OF
THE SITE BEING A PLANET WHICH THEN HAS MOONS AND
SATELLITES.

is what we were used to. The formatting of early television programmes was based on the 'staged' appearance of theatre, because we felt safe within the limits of something we knew. Most CD–ROM titles today are little more than books read using VCR controls — two familiar, domesticated technologies — and this demonstrates that when faced with any new technology, we revert to an aping of a previous technology because we feel threatened by it. Here we see the equivalent of a reversal trend in architecture, that of 'Veneer Vernacular', or the need to dress up a modernistic or futuristic approach behind a facade of familiarity. The advent of the book itself was seen as a threat, and its potential for mass education was perceived as a direct challenge

we have seen arguments against amateur DTP and DTV — but, inevitably, the computer will enhance the possibilities of the distribution of information, and it will enable anyone to have hands–on use of the tools of communication, previously restricted to a series of elite groups whose main intention was the safeguarding of their trade.

Electronic publishing first found support in education. It was perceived as a powerful tool for the dissemination of information. This channel has now come to be regarded as the prime target of entertainment providers, whose ambition is to exploit and feed the addictive nature of multimedia for its own end. The danger of localised media being suffocated by homogeneity is very real. Electronic publishing provides a vital network for individualised communication, of being able to publish ideas and thoughts that would not normally be given the time of day on any major network or in any major publication. It reverses the trend of mass media, splintering monosyllabic multinational chunks of information into personalised and humanistic messages. We are now witnessing the birth of a kind of independent movement within electronic publishing, similar to the move towards independence in the record industry. It is there that we must look for hope and inspiration. It is only there that we can find a mental approach capable of challenging our preconceptions and limitations and a

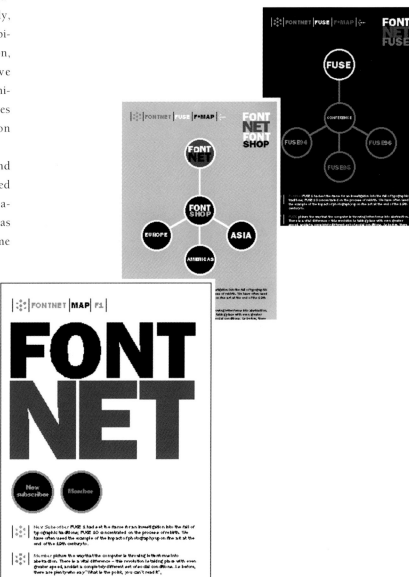

RESEARCH ARTS TRIED TO DEVELOP A DESIGN FOR THE
SITE WHICH IS PURPOSE BUILT FOR DISPLAY ON THE
INTERNET, INSTEAD OF TAKING A LANGUAGE WHICH HAS
BEEN CREATED FOR PRINT AND THEN ADAPTED TO AN
ON–LINE PUBLICATION. THEY EMPLOYED 'BISM' – BIG
IMPACT, SMALL MEMORY – BECAUSE THEY FEEL THAT MOST
SITES ARE BUILT WITHOUT KEEPING IN MIND THE ACTUAL
MODEM POSSIBILITIES THAT PEOPLE HAVE.

The Cultural Challenge of Interactive Hypermedia
Is there a future for the book?

With the emergence of new media in publishing, many have begun to ask worried questions about the future of the book. In this essay I will argue that the physical object 'book' has been disappearing since printing was invented, that the concept 'book' will never disappear, and that the coming century will see the production of whole new interactive, non–linear products of great cultural significance.

In debates about the book's future, two completely different issues are generally confused. People are scared that their bibliophile copies of Anna Karenina will be taken away from them or that they will be forced for the rest of their lives to read the screens of automatic bank teller machines or play video games. I don't believe this for a moment. Books are an indispensable vehicle for our culture and have acquired a solid market position since their invention. People like to read and write books. The carefully composed linear narration that finds its intimate refuge in books corresponds so beautifully to the course of our lives that there will always be a large group of people who identify wholly with them.

What rabid defenders of the printed book miss, however, is that the physical presence of books has been crumbling away for more than five centuries. Since the invention of printing —

sive and heavy to take along when one was travelling. A rightful criticism, but one which also must be considered in the context of development.

Our literary culture exists only by the grace of the mass–produced book. Our literary activity

took nearly a thousand years for the first story to be written down. That moment corresponded roughly (give or take a century) to the transition from hieroglyphs to cuneiform. That was a technical innovation. In retrospect, we can hardly say whether it was

often falsely seen as the beginning of book culture — the book has been disappearing. Compare the material presence of a medieval manuscript with that of a twentieth-century novel — especially the mass-marketed paperback version. The book's evaporation has seen the growth of the number of books produced while the price declined spectacularly. And the readability and usability of books has increased greatly. The disappearance of the physical book has been a pre-condition for centuries for the growth of book culture.

It doesn't take much imagination to see how this development will continue into the next century. Of course, books will become electronic, but only if the electronic books become more readable, easier to use and cheaper than paper books. That will take time: ten years for the necessary technical development and then roughly another ten to get over our initial hesitation. In a quarter of a century, the paper book will have become an expensive collector's item, like the parchment book now.

Today's first, clumsy attempts at electrification of books have rightfully met with criticism. Of crucial importance is the emergence of computers with which we can read the electronic books. At the moment, they are too big, too expensive, they hum, they have ugly letters and are anchored to the wall with an electric cord. However, the readability of today's letters on the screen is excellent compared with Gutenberg's headache typography. His broken letters dominated German typography until far into this century and are a prime example of bad readability. Yet, they did not halt the rise of the book. Today's critique is actually comparable to that of a citizen of Mainz in the middle of the fifteenth century, who complained to Gutenberg that the bibles he was printing were too expen-

today is entirely determined by the technological means offered by our culture. We have all been raised by readers of books to be readers of books. For the young person filled with the urge to create, nothing could be more natural than writing a book! Today's novelist may have become a minstrel six hundred years ago. Or a court jester.

When the Sumerians began to write four thousand years before Christ, it wasn't to write down stories, but to balance their accounts. It

fuelled by the cultural need to write down existing stories, or culture simply made eager use of the new technique it was offered.

The ancient intelligentsia resisted the modern technique of writing long and persistently. Socrates was of the opinion (written down anyway by his hard-headed student Plato) that writing could be nothing more than a memory aid: You writers provide your followers with a sort of wisdom that is not based on reality, because the large amount of information that they can absorb without any form of counsel will give them the feeling that they have acquired a great deal of knowledge, while in fact they still know absolutely nothing. And they will also become offensive people because they will merely believe themselves to be wise...

Just as the writing down of stories was made possible by the misuse of accounting tools and literature only gathered momentum when text began to be mechanically reproducible on a large scale, we can now be certain that art will take over the new media now emerging. (By the way, the application that led to the breakthrough of the personal computer in the early eighties was the calculating program Lotus 123...)

In the meantime, we have outgrown the book phase and computers are being used increasingly to write texts,

The following comparison might serve to indicate how dramatic the social influence of this development really is: the video game company Nintendo now has a larger yearly turnover than the entire record industry at its height in the seventies.

Computers are everywhere and it is naive to imagine that they will not increasingly be used as a vehicle for art and culture. Young people filled with the urge to create in the next century will simply think of a computer before they think of a book. We may find this a cause for concern, like Socrates or the cultural pessimists of this fin de siècle. We might also worry a bit less and try and grasp the specific possibilities of the computer medium.

At this point, it is very difficult to say what the new culture will be like. But if we assume that art always uses the means available, perhaps by extension we can predict some of the impending developments. I want to attempt to understand what the key characteristics of the medium computer are and how they can be applied to making art.

Electronic hypertext can be seen as the externalisation of the reading technique of an erudite person, a next step in the evolution of the written word. For the author, the dynamic connection of texts (and images and sounds), organised in a non-linear fashion, might be a means of tightening the grip on the reader. And it is precisely there that the new, exciting possibilities of digital culture lie. Computers offer authors a way to tighten their grip on the reader. The writers of coming generations will not only make use of them because the technology is available, but because they offer a way to make meaningful statements in our culture, which is characterised by an overabundance of text. The

most monumental written hypertext *avant la lettre* is Walter Benjamin's Passagenwerk. Benjamin understood that history could no longer be one story and devoted more than ten years of his life to his non-linear history of the nineteenth century. The Passagenwerk is an immense structure of 'samples' that he revealed using the architectonic metaphor of the nineteenth-century 'shopping mall'. It is only now, a half-century later, that the technical means for this writing of context have become available.

Just as the introduction of printing allowed literary culture to flourish, computers will be the bearers of hyperculture. And the question of whether culture motivates technological devel-

Occasionally, I even am moved and inspired by original digital work, unexpected for someone who is almost forty years old and educated in book production and art history. I have not exactly yet been moved to tears whilst browsing a CD-ROM or web site. But I have been touched. It is a start.

It will take a lot of time for hyperculture to grow up. Reading and writing context is so new that only very few are capable of enjoying it. This is not only a matter of the emergence of conventions and comprehension of one's surroundings. In my view, that is too simple a conception. The development of the aesthetics of hypertext will take generations and will be

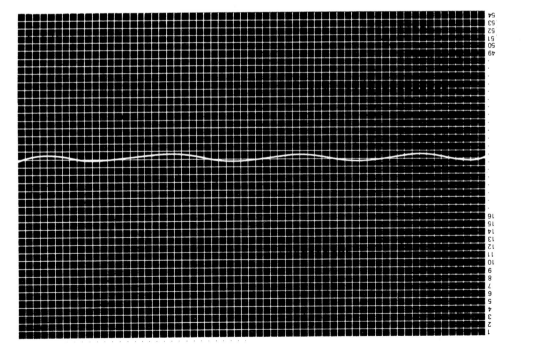

THE TABULA RASA OF THE VISICALC SCREEN. THE LATE NINETEEN-SEVENTIES SPREADSHEET PROGRAM VISICALC WAS THE PREDECESSOR OF LOTUS 123, THE "KILLER APPLICATION" THAT PUT THE PERSONAL COMPUTER ON EVERY CORPORATE DESKTOP. AS IN THE DAYS OF THE INVENTION OF WRITING, THE NEW TECHNOLOGY WAS FIRST USED FOR ACCOUNTING. THIS BOOK SHOWS OUR FIRST ATTEMPTS TO DO SOMETHING CULTURALLY SIGNIFICANT WITH IT. COMPARED TO THE THOUSAND YEARS THE SUMERIANS TOOK TO MAKE THAT TRANSITION, WE'RE NOT DOING TOO BAD. NO REASON FOR IMPATIENCE.

preceding hundred years have seen an increasing displacement of the meaning and aesthetics of art to the context instead of the content. The contentual acts of the artists migrate from the text itself to the connections that they establish between texts.

This is a general social tendency which is not only evident in art. The pessimist George Steiner, for example, calls attention to the emergence of something he calls secondary culture: text about text. This book is a good example. What Steiner and others still refuse to understand is that this is not the rise of a secondary culture, but of a hyperculture. They entirely miss the aesthetic and contentual possibilities of this development, while enough respectable examples exist in our own century. As Norbert Bolz writes, the most important books of the twentieth century are hypertext *avant la lettre* — and that is not true only of books.

The best example might be the work of Marcel Duchamp. When he signed a urinal and exhibited it in a gallery, it was an artistic act of which the significance and the beauty were completely contained in the object's relationship to the context. The text itself, the urinal, was meaningless and ugly. The actual work of art was Duchamp's act. Only visual art can say so much with such a simple act. Writers need more words to do that.

opment or vice–versa is still as difficult to answer as it was five thousand years ago.

The first steps are being taken now. I have used electronic reference works on CD–ROM and Internet while writing this article. The electronic reference work is gaining ground. It is cheaper, contains more and is easier to use than its paper predecessors. The Voyager Company in New York has an extensive collection of classic, linear titles on floppy disk. Some of our computer games contain as much text as a good–sized novella. Already, most of Mediamatic's work consists of preparing digital titles.

accompanied by extensive changes of consciousness, comparable to literature's long development, which took place in continual exchange with much broader social developments. However, I would advise no–one to have great expectations for the nearest future. And hyperculture will never replace book culture; hypertext exists by grace of text.

Willem Velthoven

Readability was not a prime criterion for the successful introduction of new media in the 15th–century. This detail of a Gutenberg Bible clearly shows the hopeless quality of early typography. It was beautiful in its graphical quality and rhythm but any screen with this kind of type would fail in the current market.

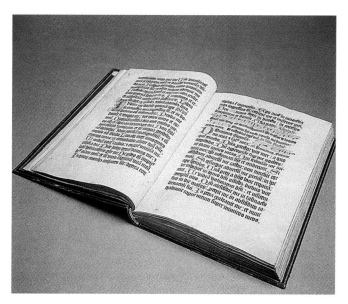

15

The book at the beginning of its disappearance. This 15th–century Bible was printed by one of Gutenberg's pupils. It was too heavy to carry around and too expensive as well. The book you are reading now represents the upper quality level of mass market books in this century. Yet, next to this predecessor it seems flimsy. You only have to compare this impressive piece to a contemporary pocket book to understand where things are heading…

Interaction Design
State of the Art and Future Developments
An argument for information design

Everybody is complaining about an epidemic of information overload, but people don't seem to realise that the resulting information fatigue is largely a functional design problem. To whit: good design makes information visible and manageable, but we are still at a very early stage in our understanding of information design. We are all whining about crude screen designs, hierarchical menus, and maze–like hypermedia structures, whereas we need to start by addressing the general question of dynamic information design. In this paper, I argue that interface design and computer graphics should transmute into a discipline I would refer to as 'information design'. Good information design will offer us the means to manage both new media and new paradigms of communication.

It is not the quantity of available data that has triggered the electronic gold rush on the Internet, but rather the enhanced accessibility of the system through the World Wide Web. The Web is more than simply a new representation of information on–line. While much of the information was out there for years, most people couldn't access it in a practical and attractive way. It was the advent of the Web's browsing systems and their graphic

the interface becomes the target of our design efforts. This separation leads to a break between the superficial design and the functional definition of the object. While this is an accepted situation with transportation designs – cars are physical objects, after all – industrial design for

GEORGES MELIES SHOT HIS THEATRE PIECES WITH A STATIC CAMERA IN 1895 FROM AN EXTERNAL POINT OF VIEW. BY ADDING CAMERA MOTION THE OPERATOR OF THE CAMERA ENTERS THE VIRTUAL SPACE OF THE FILM (CF. WALTER BENJAMIN OP. CIT.). NEW MEDIA ARE CAPABLE OF ENTERING THE SPACE OF THE PRINTED BOOK AND SHOWING US THE WORLD THROUGH THE TEXT. (DISCUSSION WITH SARAH HAHN, 1995, BOOKS FROM INSIDE– BOOKS FROM OUTSIDE, ART CENTER COLLEGE OF DESIGN, PASADENA CA.)

virtual objects needs to be delineated. As new media have no actual, physical presence in the world, the creative impulse is thus required to design the invisible. In turn, a new understanding of the communicative is needed.

was still a multi–purpose tool: you shot the film with it, and you projected with the same machine. The projector and the films themselves were limited in size by the power of the lamp as well as time by the length of the celluloid. With the exception of the fact that the recording as well as the projection was hand––cranked, all limitations apply — *mutatis mutandis* — to the development of dynamic media on the computer.

There is a fundamental duality to new media: the computer is both a tool of creation and a delivery platform. In many ways, the field of 'computer graphics' suffers from a split personality: the term covers all sorts of application and media. While the usage of the computer to define a graphic representation is a dramatic step away from classic graphic design, the use of the computer as a tool says little about the necessities of conceptual design of an interactive piece. For this, we require a new branch of object design: we need to devise an immaterial architecture for the virtual information environments.

How this immaterial architecture manifests itself technically, and in what medium it does so, is not as major an issue as it appears. The

THE PLASTIC LID USED IN THE US TO CARRY AROUND COFFEE SAFELY IS A GOOD EXAMPLE OF HOW THE PRIMARY EXPERIENCE IS DISTURBED BY A TECHNICAL INTERFACE. THE COVER AS INTERFACE NEEDS TO TELL YOU WHERE AND HOW TO DRINK, A TASK WE HAD MANAGED AT THE AGE OF TWO.

Design is always also a grounding process that relates the object to the world we live in. The task of designing the ungraspable has gained in importance throughout the history of representational technologies: from photography to the cinema and television, and now with computer–generated media. New media address a Gestalt that is different from other media while drawing from the functional experiences of the media types they rely on. One would expect that what we call new media should be called modern media but the media in question are far less defined by their theoret-

representation that transformed the Internet from a pipeline of academic data into the much over-hyped Information Superhighway. And while pioneers on the last frontier register their claim in Cyberspace, designers are asked to turn the free flow of information into selected media for specific purposes.

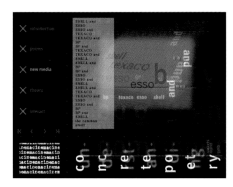

THE TRANSITION FROM PAPER TO THE DYNAMIC MEDIUM OF THE SCREEN CHALLENGES THE WRITTEN TEXT. BY EXPERIMENTING WITH ELEMENTS OF CONCRETE POETRY WHICH IN ITSELF HOLDS A DIALECTIC PROCESS OF TEXT AND GRAPHIC REPRESENTATION, TYPOGRAPHY BECOMES DYNAMIC. (THOMAS MÜLLER, 1995, UNDERSTANDING CONCRETE POETRY, CD-ROM, ART CENTER COLLEGE OF DESIGN, PASADENA CA.)

These new forms in turn will create new types of media, dramatically different from what we call new media or multimedia today. These media will be driven by the information they convey and no longer by the technology they use. They will also be far more diversified than 'multimedia'.

The design fallacy

Today the field of *Design* is widely conceived of as 'graphic' design of the surface and – in the case of new media – the interface. The interface is seen to be the gate through which the content within the new medium can be accessed. Thus,

How new is the new medium?

In 1959, Jean Cocteau wrote : *'Vive la jeune muse cinéma, car elle possède le mystère du rêve et permet de rendre l'irréalité réaliste.'* Film had finally become accepted as art, collected for its design and its narrative. After the 100-year reign of film, we seem to be back on the frontier, pioneering the aesthetics of multimedia. But, again, what we call the New Multimedia are neither new nor media — they are a conglomeration of technologies (hence multi–) used to define new communication channels. Yet, these channels lack the necessary paradigms of informational flow and audience involvement of traditional media.

The computer — especially the personal computer — has served as an important step towards a unified communication paradigm, but it was never conceived of as a communication technology, nor, even more importantly, as a platform to convey ideas. We therefore have had to take considerable effort to turn the calculating machine first into a typewriter, and then into a communication device. After many detours, we may feel that things have sorted themselves out. But, by stepping back and taking an overall view, we can quickly spot the sore points and acknowledge that the current state of multimedia technology is intermediate at best.[1]

As we implement them today, dynamic media on the computer are no more conceptually advanced than film was in 1903. At that point, film had moved away from the static recording of theatre pieces to the first development of real filmic narratives. Film was still very limited in technology, both conceptually and in terms of its integration into the social structure. In the earliest cinemas, the camera

THE INTERDEPENDENCE OF OBJECT AND THE MESSAGE CONTAINED WITHIN IS NO LONGER STABLE. FOR MARSHALL McLUHAN, THE END OF THE 'GUTENBERG GALAXY' DID NOT MEAN THE ACCEPTANCE OF NEW TECHNOLOGICAL INVENTIONS, BUT OF NON–EUCLIDIAN SPACE AS IT REDEFINES THE DIMENSIONS OF OUR PERCEPTION.

availability of the material does not define the medium, much as the physical object of paper no longer defines the conceptual category of 'book', 'periodical' or even a 'daily newspaper' [*sic*]. The decision regarding the delivery platform (paper or electronic or both) strongly influences the work, but the medium is defined by the communicative concept in conjunction with the delivery technology.

NEW MEDIA ARE CURRENTLY OBSESSED WITH RECREATING REALITY. EVERY TECHNICAL ATTEMPT IS BEING MADE TO SHOW THAT SPECIAL EFFECTS CAN DO BETTER THAN THE REAL WORLD OUT THERE (CONCEPT: FLORIAN BRODY, MONTAGE: SARAH HAHN, 1995)

ical approach than by the newness of the technology involved. Therefore we see electronic books, digital film, sampled sound, but not a fully co-ordinated new communication paradigm. To develop this, we need to address the centrality of the field of information design. And as design is already relying heavily in many fields on computers, software development influences the way things look and, to an even greater extent, the way things work. But design is not only about the graphic surface — in our case, the screen interface — but about the underlying structure. The Bauhaus legacy 'Form follows Function' can be implemented in a new way by creating the design of the function on the same platform as the design of the form. The strange metaphors of the button and the switch as triggering elements, derived from a physical object that itself is barely 100 years old, can serve as an icon for the current state of functional interface design. One is tempted to think of the huge soft plugs and switches designed by Claes Oldenburg when considering the physical quality of such objects. Yet we need to examine these metaphors on the base level: Light switches are bad enough on the wall, why would I need them on my screen? Perhaps we have to admit that even now, the new media are not so new after all, but rather a digital replication of a mechanical environment. The representation of information within such a system will always be limited and we need to go beyond these constraints to set a new standard for an artificial memory, as this is what we are really looking for.[2]

The digital catch

New media perforce demand the constant re-design of interfaces. While 'old' media did not have such an interface and could speak for themselves, electronic new media have a structure that stands between them and the user. Accordingly, digital media do not age well. While you can almost watch the design getting outdated and

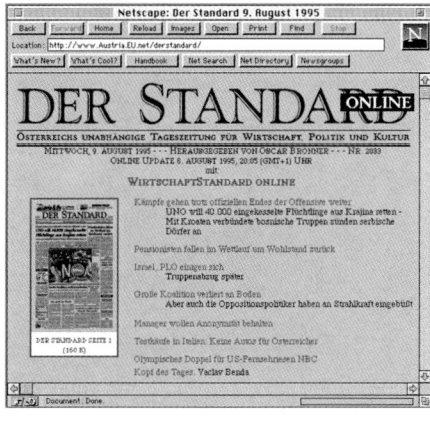

old–fashioned, the piece itself in no way builds up a patina, but due to its praised digital quality remains ever new. Even the new orange leatherette of the sixties eventually cracked. Digital pieces, on the other hand, will always be new — they cannot be stone–washed and will never have the broken–in look of a Chesterfield sofa.

What is hard to predict is whether society will encourage or discourage such developments.' [4] The future of design will be the design of information instead of the design of interfaces, inserted between the user and the information.

New Media – New Interaction – New Design

While we discuss the interactivity of the so–called new media, we forget to observe their relation to classic media, many of them equally dynamic. Books have been and are still the most interactive medium to communicate concepts. Books are now and have always been uniquely suited to be containers of ideas. Ancient traditions structure the way we create and utilise the technology of the book. The <u>Ars Memorativa</u> of the Romans assigned places to images, created maps to reconstruct the structure and content of narrative. The book followed suit, creating a storehouse of picture and story, bound between covers.

The German media theorist Norbert Bolz is convinced that the *information processing system 'book' is clearly no longer up to the complexity of our social systems. The New Media unfold the grey environment of text into the spectral colours of sensuous knowledge.* [5] The common experience that the film was not as good as the book proves that the colours in the mind of the reader can be far more seductive than the best Technicolor. The amount of data gathered for digestion is definitely larger but this is a design problem we have to solve soon, not a book problem. The book will move from the paper page to the dynamic electronic medium as it moved from papyrus to paper.

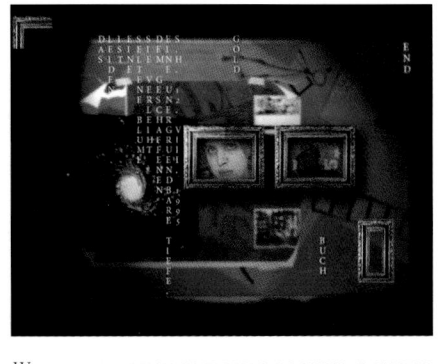

"Well, this certainly buggers our plans to conquer the Universe."

WELL, THIS CERTAINLY BUGGERS…

becomes the third of the series of operators described by Walter Benjamin[7] in 1936: the film camera operator and the operating surgeon. Both enter deep into the tissue of reality when doing the work, while the magical healer and the painter both keep a distance from their objects. Bolz concedes that true hypertext is a rhizome which requires a self–assertive user, but it remains unclear if this true hypertext can come up to all the expectations to solve the omnipresent information overload.

WHILE INFORMATION IN ELECTRONIC MEDIA IS MOSTLY MEASURED BY ITS EFFICIENCY, SIZE AND SPEED, THIS POEM EXPLORES THE EMOTIONAL SPACE OF THE SCREEN. SARAH HAHN WRITES: DAS LEIDEN IST EINE SELTENE BLUME, SIE VERLEIHT DEM GESCHAFFENEN EINE UNERGRÜNDBARE TIEFE. (SORROW IS A RARE FLOWER WHICH ADDS UNFATHOMABLE DEPTH TO THE CREATED.)

Eventually, a history of digital media will develop and we will see organic developments. For now, we don't even know how to preserve and collect these pieces (another situation we have encountered with film). The definition of a future requires a past and we can already see a temporal development of different representations of dynamic media.

New media are only new until they are no longer new — and old in this context always means accepted and established. Therefore, we see a continuous process of rejuvenation and the new media are those that almost work. So new media have this Dorian Grey–like quality: they never age. Being described and re–described in more or less professional periodicals in the field of technology and design, they need to be 'cutting edge' and 'state–of–the–art'.[3] New media become outdated very fast and with this continuous retiring process of the technology, the design that accompanies them becomes old–fashioned with equal speed.

So what will the future bring?

The dynamic representation of information on a screen will no longer be new media, and the interface paradigm will disappear. Bob Stein, the co–founder of the Voyager Company, argued for this point in an on–line discussion about electronic books. *'Perhaps the biggest problem with predicting the trajectory of a given technology is that it resides within a broader social context. It might be easy to imagine how the Internet could help "break down the traditional power relationship between author and reader" or vastly expand the number of authors relative to the number of readers.*

DON'T TRY THIS AT HOME.

Bolz argues that the meaning of an electronic text is its use in the respective reading matter, a fact that holds true in all aspects for language across media.[6] And the computer spawns the electronic text, a volatile form that paradoxically returns the text to our heads while at the same time enmeshing it in an even more sophisticated apparatus. Through its digitalisation, it no longer rests in the universe of original and reproduction but transcends to a state where every reproduction is an original. Thus the user of the PC

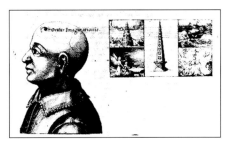

THE CLASSIC 'ART OF MEMORY' ASSUMED THAT A VISUAL REPRESENTATION OF THE OUTSIDE WORLD COULD BE STORED IN A REAL ENVIRONMENT AND LATER RECALLED BY OFFERING RULES FOR PLACES AND RULES FOR IMAGES. (FRANCES YATES, THE ART OF MEMORY, HAMMONDSWORTH, PENGUIN, 1978).

Conclusion

We can no longer tolerate boundaries in the field of graphic design. Today, 'information design' must begin to absorb different disciplines. As it moves from the beautification of screen layouts to the definition of communicative concepts, the field of design gains a new position in the definition of media. What we call new media are not so much new media, nor even new technology . Instead, they are a new way to use a technology as a means of communication. But as the newness wears off, new media as an entity will give way to different forms of dynamic communication. In the discourse over the independence of these first truly invisible media, we need to address the basic notion of what it means to communicate when physical representation is in no way related to the shaping of information. The dynamic medium we see emerging today is neither 'multi' nor 'new', but the next step in the definition of our memory and the way we perceive the world. At the different levels on which design is involved in the creation of this dynamic medium, it must address both its surface as well as its functionality as a means of communication.

FLORIAN BRODY

[1] In the twenties, record players were connected to film projectors by flexible shafts to assure synchronous projection of image and sound, a technology that did not prevail. Looking at my standard multimedia set–up, I have similar feelings; there is still a direct relation between the complexity of multimedia and the amount of cables needed to connect the parts.

[2] Yates, Frances, The Art of Memory, Harmondsworth,Penguin, 1978, p. 22.

[3] A term coined by the hi–fi industry in the sixties to describe this phenomenon of 'as new — i.e., as good — as it can get'.

[4] Bob Stein in Page vs. Pixel, dialogue at FEED, July 1995, http://www.emedia.net/feed/95.05dialog2.html

[5] Bolz, Norbert, The Deluge of Sense, speech at Doors of Perception, Amsterdam 1993. Transcribed on the DopRom CD–ROM, Mediamatic, Amsterdam, 1994.

[6] Wittgenstein, Ludwig, Philosophical Investigations.

[7] Benjamin, Walter,The work of art in the age of mechanical reproduction. In Illuminations, New York, Schocken. 1969. First published in Zeitschrift für Sozialforschung. V. 1, 1936.

How to Make a CD-ROM in Three Easy Steps

Some general remarks and a case: Doors of Perception 1

Interactive media design is a very exciting field because it offers several new challenges to any person involved in production. It is also a risky field — accepting those challenges means dealing with a lot of unanswered questions, an open-ended production cycle and the chance of failure.

This article will deal with some of the issues involved in CD-ROM design and production. Apart from a short introduction about the composition of a good team, I will also treat on design and production methodology.

The examples and illustrations are from Doors of Perception 1, a CD-ROM produced by Mediamatic in 1994. Doors 1 was our first full-blown CD-ROM project. It is currently used as a model of good interactive media design in schools and universities around the world and it has won several international prizes. It was also a very tough learning experience. We lost quite a lot of money on it.

Here is a chance to learn from our mistakes...

Building a team

If you want to make a CD-ROM that looks like other CD-ROMs, it is probably good to find people with a lot of experience in CD-ROM-making. However, if you are aiming at

unlikely that you will be able to foresee all the details, problems and opportunities you will have to deal with. Changing decisions made in an early phase of the process can easily develop into something known as "creeping elegance", i.e., the continuous, unstructured changing and improvement of a project during later design and production stages. Because these elegant changes creep in on a case-by-case basis (and usually under stressful conditions of production), they do not necessarily improve the product as a whole. They occur in various, separate stages and tend to be impossible to implement throughout the whole project. This causes them to ultimately have a negative effect on the consistency of the design. They also tend to drive production beyond all deadlines and budgets.

The best way to avoid creeping elegance is to plan some iterations in the development process right from the beginning. After agreeing on a concept, do a short run of quick design exercises. Then, re-evaluate the concept with the first sketches on the table. You will probably be able to improve on the clarity and precision of the concept. This also offers a second opportunity to check your ideas with the client. This will prepare you to embark on the more detailed, but also more focused design phase, during which you'll have to make fewer and

In the case of Doors 1, the answers were:

1. About the Doors of Perception 1 conference. The goal was to deliver the twenty-odd lectures in a multimedia format and to capture the conference in its most attractive and valuable aspects.

2. More then an overview of who spoke and what they said, we wanted to capture something of the atmosphere of the event, the issues, the opposing points of view.

3. We did expect the users to have a rather varied and unsystematic interest in the subject matter of the conference. So we decided we had to find a way to use the users' personal involvement with the various issues to drive the interaction.

Of course, the development of the concept is not something that can be done without already considering more detailed editorial issues and questions. One also has to consider the target group, other titles in the same market, etcetera. But it is of utmost importance to formulate these answers as early in the process as possible.

One then can proceed with stage two.

THE 'OOPS' BUTTON WAS OUR MOST DIFFICULT VICTORY OVER OUR SYSTEM THINKING. THIS SIMPLE DEVICE THAT TAKES THE USER ONE STEP BACK IS REDUNDANT FOR ANY PERSON THAT FULLY GRASPS THE INFORMATION STRUCTURE OF THE CD. IT TOOK US A WHILE TO REALISE THAT WE WOULD BE THE ONLY USERS EVER TO OVERSEE THE SYSTEM OF OUR OWN PRODUCTION.

AFTER SOME USER TESTING WE DISCARDED ANY BACKTRACKING DEEPER THAN THIS ONE STEP. THE ONLY OTHER RECORD OF THE MOVEMENTS OF A USER THROUGH THE CD IS A FULL ONE THAT CAN BE PRINTED AFTER PLAYING THE DISK.

producing something innovative, it is probably better to look for talented professionals from the various disciplines that will constitute your media mix.

For most productions, you will need a sound designer, an interaction designer, a typographer, a graphic/animation artist, a programmer, an editor/writer and a production manager. Of course, if you find some multi-talents or consider yourself one, you can reduce the number of staff.

For Doors of Perception, the various team members had been involved across the board in making books, magazines, film, music, games, television, fine art and exhibitions. This broad professional and cultural background proved very useful during the project.

Depending on your design and content, you might need production staff for image editing, digital sound and video post-production, multimedia authoring, screen lay-out, and sub-editing text.

Structuring the project

As in any other medium, a project falls into three stages: concept, design and production. Although design exercises can inform the concept development process considerably, it is advisable to try and separate design and concept development as much as possible. The same goes for production and design. During the production of Doors 1, we made changes in design during the production process. These changes turned out to be extremely costly and forced us to produce parts of the CD all over again — a frustrating exercise for everyone involved.

However, when you aim to make a very high quality product, these dilemmas cannot always be avoided. When you are not developing the second or third title in a series, it is

much more detailed prototypes. You will also win time to test production methods, an important part of the design work. Because this phase is more focused and thorough, it will be easier to stick to your decisions during production.

By anticipating and leaving some room for your changes of mind, you will be able to avoid the frustration and unforeseeable delays of later changes.

Stage one: Concept

Since interactive multimedia is far more complex in structure than any linear product, a clear concept is of utmost importance. Client, editors, designers and production staff have to know what the goal of the project is and every decision has to be based on it. This doesn't mean that the concept cannot be tweaked during the process, but changing it is very time-consuming and expensive, because one basically has to re-think every single decision based on the old concept. When one doesn't know exactly where the production has to go, it will probably end up going nowhere and become a bag of compromises where design doesn't support content properly, and where the user is unable to figure out what the title is really about because the makers didn't really know themselves.

The basic question is very simple: What will it be about? The second question is: What do we want to give the user? What do we want to say about the subject? The third question should be: What is the user interested in? Which interests will drive the user through the product?

Within the constraints of time, budget, technology and available talent, all further editorial and design decisions can be directly based on the answers to the three questions above.

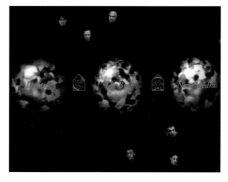

21

ONLY ONE THIRD OF THE DOORS HOME SCREEN, THE CENTRAL NAVIGATION AREA, IS VISIBLE AT ONE TIME. WHEN THE MOUSE POINTER IS MOVED TO THE LEFT OR RIGHT EDGE OF THE SCREEN, IT SCROLLS IN THE OPPOSITE DIRECTION. AUDIO FEEDBACK IS PROVIDED BY RAISING THE PITCH OF THE BACKGROUND NOISE OF THIS AREA, THE SOFT MUMBLING OF A CONFERENCE AUDIENCE.

THE GREENHOUSE SHAPES ARE BUTTONS THAT TAKE THE USER TO SECONDARY INFORMATION LIKE CREDITS, RECOMMENDED READING OR INFORMATION ABOUT THE DESIGN INSTITUTE. THEIR FUNCTION IS EXPLAINED BY A TEXT THAT APPEARS ON ROLL OVER.

THE LITTLE FACE ICONS PROVIDE DIRECT ACCESS TO INDIVIDUAL SPEAKERS' DOCUMENTATION. THERE ARE NO WRITTEN NAMES OF THE SPEAKERS HERE, JUST THEIR FACES AND THE SOUND OF THEIR VOICES ON ROLL OVER. ALTHOUGH THE 22 FACES ARE SCATTERED IN ALPHABETICAL ORDER FROM LEFT TO RIGHT, WE DECIDED THAT A SYSTEMATICAL ACCESS TO THE SPEAKERS WOULD BE MORE APPROPRIATE IN A POP-UP MENU IN THE SPEAKERS' DOCUMENTATION AREA. THEIR FACES AND VOICES PLAYED A MORE IMPORTANT ROLE DURING THE CONFERENCE ITSELF AND ARE ALSO PUT IN THE FOREGROUND ON THE CD.

THE BIG ROUND SHAPES ARE THREE OF THE EIGHT 'AUDITORIUM ENTRANCES'. THEY'RE MARKED WITH A KEY WORD AND, UPON ROLL OVER, EMIT THE STATEMENT THAT OPENS THE 'DISCUSSION' BEHIND THAT ENTRANCE.

Stage two: Editorial, interaction, sound and visual design

Note that I even call the editorial process 'design'. In interactive hypermedia, editorial content is part of an interwoven structure of great complexity. It is impossible to think about content in the conventional sense of the word. The way the various linear bits of information are connected is as much part of the content as the information itself.

The lack of conventions in this very young field and the questionability of the few conventions we can distinguish at the moment make division of labour during this stage very difficult. Expect to work much harder during the development of a multimedia product.

It is insufficient for a development team to work with only a strong intuitive notion of the implications of a certain project. The team must fully grasp entire issues in all their dimensions, with each individual member able to exchange, communicate and interrelate all of his or her insights and skills, as well as to understand those of members from other disciplines.

At the start of the production of Doors, communication was difficult. The individual team members started from within their own, specific disciplines and spoke their own languages. Through striving to be teachers and students at the same time, and by devoting a lot of energy and patience to the problem, we finally developed a multi-disciplinary language that enabled us to communicate about the project. We ended up with a much closer collaboration and exchange of ideas than in productions for other media. The designers had considerable editorial input and some of the best design ideas came from the editors.

it was not necessary because the detailed and very clear navigation system of the CD allowed any place to be reached within two or three clicks anyway. What they were initially blind to was the fact that no user would ever know exactly which two or three clicks! They had difficulty imagining a user that wouldn't know their way around an information structure they knew like the back of their hands.

Too many possibilities: It was — and is — tempting to use every little trick the medium allows, but at the end of the day, designing multimedia is not about the fun of adding time, space and sound alone. It is about connections between all these things, the effects generated by the connections and the consequences that every single decision and solution can have for content and style and vice versa. What is difficult is to select the best possibilities from an endless array of options, to make decisions which show a sensible and attractive consistency, and to keep design simple and lucid.

This usually means killing a lot of nice, healthy, beautiful babies. During the development process, one typically gets ten times as many ideas as one can effectively employ in one project. The only way to decide which ideas to keep and which ones to get rid of is to test them against the original concept. Any great idea that does not directly support the concept should be discarded. When there seem to be various solutions to the same problem, one has to prototype them all and do some thorough user testing. One has to do this with single ideas as well.

Quizzes are a very popular pastime for many people. However, unless you are developing a game, it is a big mistake to assume that users

contents, index, footnotes, etcetera. After this period of training we are able to pick up a book and almost unconsciously get a very good idea of its structure, as well as the quality and quantity of its contents. The book is a very mature medium and all books work in roughly the same optimised way. Our culture and way of thinking are themselves determined by the way books work.

We're trained to understand the world as a linear, diachronically coherent collection of causes and effects. Our media provide us with random access to their content, but we always expect to be somewhere on a line.

The non–linear information structure of hypermedia blows the good old order to bits. Time becomes reversible and cause and effect can suddenly switch places. And that is what we want, because we understand that that more closely resembles certain aspects of our world. Hypermedia are a very powerful way of dealing with this. But we're just beginning. We still have to develop our tools and grow confident in working with the new media. In a sense, developing interactive multimedia is like making books for children. We are actually children designing books for children, because we ourselves are beginners too.

We are forced to experiment as designers and as users. These are very exciting times, and they will remain exciting until far into the next century when the best approaches will have emerged and be recognised as such.

SPQR: four traps to avoid

There are four dangerous traps to watch out for in multimedia development: system thinking, too many possibilities, quiz and too much room.

System thinking is an attitude that has been common in graphic design for years and that is now often seen in new media design. Basically, what happens is that the designers of a project start to assume that the users of their product are interested in the system behind it. They even expect users to understand the system. This misunderstanding is caused by the fact that, during the development of a multimedia title, there has to be a strong focus on structure. Designers are trained to think systematically. Because they are immersed in the structure and the system of the project very intensely for a long period of time, they tend to forget that users are often not very analytical in their approach to the work and sometimes spend only a few hours with it. The system of production should not necessarily be part of their experience. This means that the logic of interaction is not the logic of the information structure at all.

During the development of Doors of Perception, for instance, we had big fights about the implementation of the so-called 'Oops Button'. The Oops Button is an omnipresent button that takes the user one step back in the interaction, similar to the 'Undo' command in many application programmes. Such a provision is very comfortable for users wandering in the proverbial dark of an interactive environment. It puts the user at ease because (s)he knows that any step taken can be reversed immediately. The team members that had to implement the Oops Button objected fiercely to this rather tedious job. They claimed

are always interested in solving riddles. Or, by the same token, in 'exploring' interfaces and information structures. Very often we see multimedia interfaces that expect users to understand the function of large collections of proprietary icons. Even the word processing applications of today have 'button bars' that look very functional but are actually unintelligible to most common users.

Another kind of quiz game that better be avoided is the use of 'hot spots' on the screen. The user is expected to click on interesting parts of an image to trigger some action. These solutions always seem logical to designers because they know where they put the spots and they know what action to expect. To users these creative tricks are mainly frustrating. If they want something from the application, they want it immediately. No guessing.

In Doors of Perception we used a lot of hidden controls to keep screen design as simple as possible. We avoided the dreaded quiz by always putting those controls in the same place on every screen so it is very easy for the user to learn to find them. Whenever a user clicks on a spot that's not hot — conditioned by many other designs to look for hidden buttons— the screen immediately reveals all hidden controls; the guessing is over at first attempt.

Related to the quiz trap is the eternal compromise between accessibility and challenge. We decided to have faith in our users' intelligence and to make our interface a bit more complex and powerful.

This conflict between direct comprehensibility and a powerful interface is something that will plague interaction designers for decades to come. At school, we learn the alphabet, grammar, analytical reading and a lot of handy conventions like page numbers, table of

So at the moment we cannot afford to design for obviousness. That would limit us to existing conventions. On the other hand, there is no point in pushing development beyond comprehensibility. We must compromise. This places CD-based interactive media somewhere between computer games and location–based applications such as kiosks. Games invariably have a high challenge component in their design. The player wants to master the game. But, once mastered, it becomes uninteresting. Location-based interaction, such as point-of-sale information systems and possibly interactive TV, on the other hand, has to deliver immediately. The user doesn't have time to learn any new skills. In designing this CD we assumed that we could expect the user to spend at least some time familiarising him– or herself with it.

The final trap I have to point out is a very simple one: CD-ROMs and, even more, the internet have seemingly unlimited capacity. There's just too much room; no extra charge for colour printing nor for a couple of extra pages. In old media the size of a project is naturally constrained by the physical size of the final product. In multimedia these

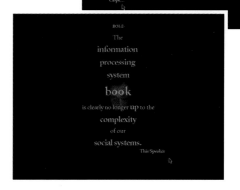

constraints have to be consciously self-imposed. It's very easy to add all kinds of layers and extra information during the concept stage. We're happy to tell the client about all the great things we're going to include in the product. Only at later stages one discovers that the design and production work to fill all this free space can be very costly and time consuming. In Doors we ended up designing more than 2000 screens and administering more than 8000 links. The disk became an incredibly rich reference work but we ended up with a lot of extra stress and no private life during the extended production period we brought upon ourselves by not properly calculating the consequences of our conceptual decisions at an earlier stage.

Doors, general structure 1:
Speakers' documentation

In the rest of this article I'll discuss the design of Doors of Perception 1 more in depth. We ended up dividing the contents of this CD-ROM into three main categories. One of these is the conventional proceedings. This section contains the raw material that came out of the conference: the texts of the lectures, biographical notes about the speakers, some additional papers. We organised these on a speaker-by-speaker basis, basically providing access to the material in alphabetical order.

In this section, we didn't really try to exploit the possibilities of the electronic book. There is no way for the user to make notes in the text, there are no cross-references, one cannot even copy a paragraph and paste it into a word processor. Given our limited time and budget, it was simply impossible. But there were also design considerations that made us choose not to use, for instance, Voyager's excellent Expanded Book Toolkit for this part of the CD. We wanted to go

After a short period of desperation, we decided to stop trying to be faithful to the material and to the internal structure of each and every presentation. We just took bits and pieces, opinions and insights, and used them for our own purposes. With these loose bits, we created a discussion that never 'really' took place at the conference. At first, this idea seemed very irresponsible to us, as decent, academically trained people. But, after a while, it seemed only natural.

The structure we developed for organising these discrete samples of the conference is that of a discussion. It is a group of people having a conversation that is very interactive: someone says something, another adds to it or perhaps strongly disagrees. Often, someone brings up an idea that is slightly beside the point and others pick up on it, thus leading the discussion in new directions.

The discussion model turned out to be very powerful in establishing connections within the basically incoherent collection of utterances we were dealing with. After testing a few variations, we developed a maze of disagreements, agreements and more indifferent relations — the three basic kinds of relationship in any discussion. The maze is constructed according to a very simple set of rules: each node branches out in exactly these three directions. After a rather intensive period of fitting all the pieces together, we had a system that could be explored again and again in an unlimited number of ways, always generating a new discourse on the fly. We created multiple entrances to the discussion that could be labelled with keywords and we finally managed to avoid short loops in the structure.

Parallel to developing the information structure, we were faced with the challenge of designing an interface that would enable the user to browse in a pleasant and meaningful way. We

WHEN THE 'THIS SPEAKER' OPTION IS CHOSEN IN THE AUDITORIUM, OR WHEN A SPEAKER'S FACE IS CLICKED IN THE HOME AREA, YOU GET A "PORTRAIT OF THAT SPEAKER. THE ROW OF MOUTHS AT THE BOTTOM OF THE SCREEN ARE CLICKABLE AND TRIGGER A NUMBER OF AUDIO LOOPS. THESE 'BEAT BOX' MUSICAL PORTRAITS ARE COMPOSITIONS BASED ON A SAMPLE OF THE SPEAKER'S VOICE. THEY ARE AMONG THE MOST POPULAR PARTS OF THE CD. AGAIN, TEXTUAL INFORMATION IS MOVED TO A LOWER LEVEL OF THE INFORMATION STRUCTURE.

TO AVOID ANY QUIZ-LIKE ANNOYANCE, WE PROVIDED THE USER WITH A PEEK AT ALL HIDDEN CONTROLS WHENEVER THERE'S A CLICK IN A NON HOT SPOT AREA. ALL BUTTONS ARE EITHER CLEARLY RECOGNISABLE AS SUCH OR BECOME VISIBLE ON ROLL OVER. THIS WAY THE SCREEN BECOMES SENSITIVE TO THE USERS' EXPLORATIONS WITHOUT UNDULY FORCING HIM TO EXPERIMENT.

further beyond the conventions of the book than the Expanded Book Toolkit would ever have allowed. At the time of the production of the disk there were no authoring tools that supported more advanced visual and interaction design as well as extensive text handling. Also because our client, the Netherlands Design Institute, asked us to focus on the advanced design of the product, we had to decide to compromise on the text retrieval capabilities of the disk.

When a user clicks on a speaker's face in the Home area, a full screen portrait comes up. This portrait is not just a visual 'cover screen' for information about and from that speaker: clicking the mouth icon at the bottom of this screen enables one to hear a 'musical portrait' of each speaker. Although we couldn't resist the temptation to play around a bit with our honourable speakers' voices and physiognomies, our primary intention here was to provide clear and memorable 'images' of all the speakers.

A very important help for exploration of the disc's contents is a screen that directly provides links into the 'Auditorium' part of Doors. Each contribution of a given speaker to the intricate hyper maze in the Auditorium is summarised there and a user can follow the links directly to a place in the maze where others are discussing the same topics.

Doors, general structure 2: The Auditorium

The second part of the CD is the result of our analysis of the material. We began by looking for a way to systematically interrelate all the information we had. We soon discovered that the material itself was not systematic at all. It would have been possible to force all the content into some structure, but this would have led to a very disappointing product because of the utterly chaotic character of the collection of talks.

included an early version of this on the disc (Auditorium Sketch). It consists of a simple screen with three buttons. After listening to and/or reading a statement, the user clicks on one of these buttons: No, Don't Know or Yes. Although the interface did exactly what it was supposed to, which was to enable the user to navigate the maze, it proved unsatisfactory. Being confronted with such clear choices stopped users in their tracks. They were forced to choose!

The second prototype (Auditorium Prototype) is very similar to the final interface. We decided that we had to present the user with a wider array of less explicit choices. To quickly test this option, which actually demanded a different information structure, we removed the three buttons of the original prototype and replaced them with an icon that the user could slide from left to right on the screen. The horizontal position of the slider would then connect to a richer array of choices that would not feel like the first prototype's 'voting' model.

The proportional slider evoked very positive reactions from our testers. They quite liked to play with it. They were no longer forced to choose between things, but only to express their feelings or general attitude. This also made it much easier for them to accept what the system gave them.

We now had to adjust the information structure to provide the necessary multitude of choices. We implemented various solutions, adding more branches and introducing random factors into the mechanism, so that the actual probability of going in a certain direction would change according to the position of the slider.

When we began testing various new versions, we were astonished to discover that users couldn't tell the difference between them. Our attempts to vary the material they ran across and

give them more control went unnoticed. In retrospect, we realised that this conforms exactly to the discussion model we were using in the first place. In real-life discussions, people have an enormous choice of expressions: they can say things, they can grimace, they can make approving or disapproving noises, they can express disinterest or contempt. But their actual power over what their conversation partner is going to say next is extremely limited. Human beings are used to dealing with the limitations of other human beings, rather than with the rigid logic of a clear information structure. They like that (well, most of them, anyway). They have other words for what we have here called limitations: words like character, opinion or culture.

I have attempted here not to make a complete or comprehensive survey of basic, structural issues of design and production, but rather to simply recount some of the critical milestones of the process as experienced by one group of authors, as well as some of the implications of these developments.

I hope that by highlighting the obstacles that had to be dealt with when trying to connect the twenty-two minds of the Doors of Perception conference's speakers to each other and to users interactively, I may have shed some light on a few of the basic problems of interactive media design in general.

WILLEM VELTHOVEN

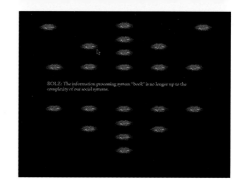

A SCREEN FROM THE FIRST SKETCH OF THE AUDITORIUM. NOT MUCH MORE IS VISIBLE THAN THE TEXT AND THE YES/DUNNO/NO BUTTONS. THIS ALL TOO CLEAR CHOICE FRUSTRATED THE USERS SO WE TRIED TO DEVELOP A MORE 'FUZZY' SOLUTION IN THE NEXT PROTOTYPE.

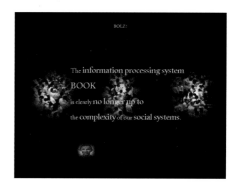

HERE IS THE SAME SCREEN FROM THE SECOND PROTOTYPE. THE SLIDER INTERFACE IS IN ITS FIRST INCARNATION. THE ONLY CHANGES WE IMPLEMENTED WERE A DIFFERENT ANIMATION AND A LEFT/RIGHT REVERSAL OF THE YES/NO POSITIONS. THE ILLUSTRATIONS WERE BLINKING DURING PLAY-BACK OF THE SPEAKER'S STATEMENT. THIS KIND OF OVER DESIGN WAS OMITTED IN THE FINAL VERSION. IT MADE CONCENTRATING ON WHAT WAS SAID MORE DIFFICULT. THE FINAL VERSION ONLY USES STILL ILLUSTRATIONS SPARSELY. MOST OF THE SCREENS JUST SHOW FACE AND TEXT, SIMPLY CENTRED. THIS DESIGN TURNED OUT TO SUPPORT THE USER'S CONCENTRATION BEST. ACTUALLY, THE ILLUSTRATIONS WE SOMETIMES USED WERE ONLY INCLUDED BECAUSE THE CONTINUED SIMPLICITY OF THE SCREENS HAD TO BE INTERRUPTED EVERY NOW AND THEN TO 'WAKE UP' THE USER.

Art & Culture

We should have mentioned before that this library is a mysterious place
where the past and the present, lives before and after death, all existing in one space.

Bio•Morph Encyclopedia Muybridge, Nobuhiro
Shibayama, 1995

In a thoroughly visual culture like ours, imagination tends to become 'imaging' — filling in ideas with pictures, imaging the world. Language is not enough anymore; we need to see before we imagine. Multimedia can be imagination in its purest possible visible form — it can resemble the chaos of images, sounds, words, noises, movements from which the imagination builds a narrative structure or a coherent whole. It can be both at the same time: a structured chaos. This may be an essence of 'original' art works on CD–ROM : imaging the imagination.

The art work's structure is associative, random if you will, and the design of a lot of multimedia art works follows John Cage's adage: no question of making understandable structures can arise; one is a tourist. It is up to the artist to lead you along well–defined paths, or to push you into a whirlpool of images and try to get hold of a raft. The design of such a work can't be neutral. As an integral part of the whole, it informs everything it carries with its own message — to a large extent, the screen design is the message. Strong graphic codes like calligraphed texts, the texture of old books, antique or modern typography and cartoon imagery are used to contextualize the work in an atmosphere of mixed metaphors and meanings. They want to be perceived in an associative way, as a work of art.

When presenting works of art in documentary multimedia, the graphic design is not so much a statement as a graceful aid to the body of art works it helps to disclose. As in art catalogues in print, cultural CD–ROMs show a preference for a modest but refined version of the modernist tradition in graphic design: clear and strong typography, a geometric use of lines and colour fields to organise the screen, a careful balancing of texts and images. But the CD–ROM can be more than just a catalogue with access to discrete bits of information; it can show the intricacies of the imaginative process almost in 'real-time' (although the brain clicks faster). By hyperlinking the art works to their sources and contexts, by confronting them with the words of the artist and by showing their different aspects in their actual surroundings, the design allows you to journey back to a state where anything was possible, before it became this collection of paintings, of sculptures, of buildings, of books.

MAX BRUINSMA

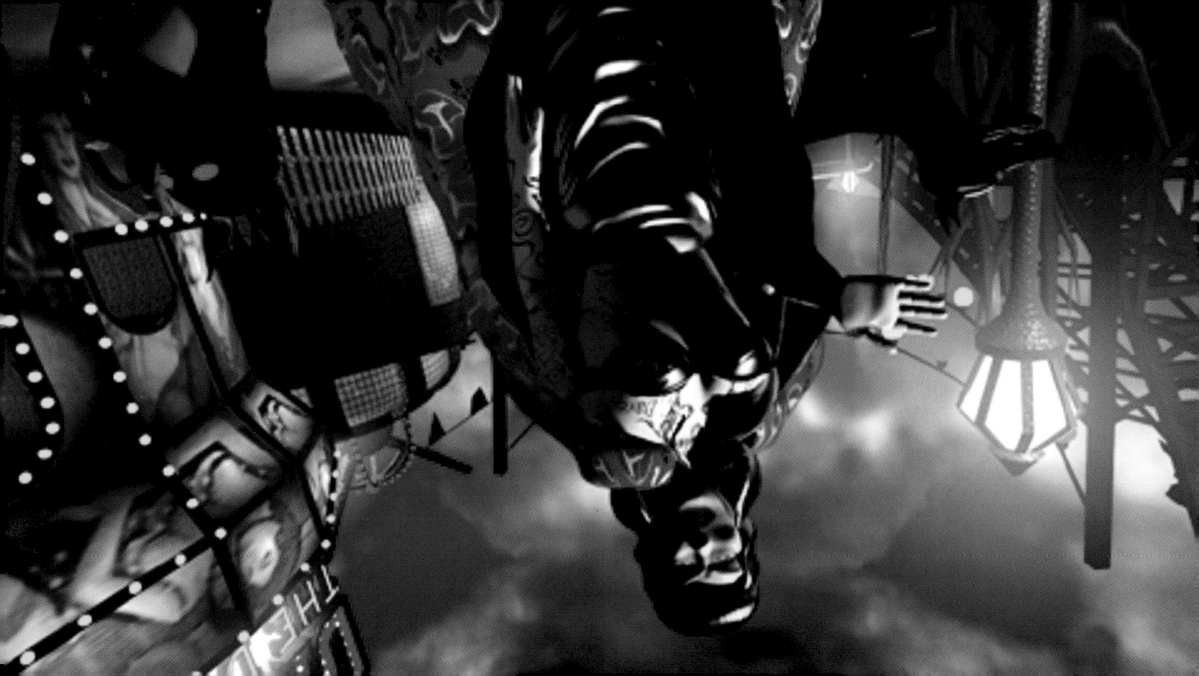

Dagmar the Dog Woman welcomes us to a scene. The combination of 3D background with keyed–in protagonists that guide us through the adventure is very similar to the approach Jim Ludtke took in Freak Show, his first production with The Residents.

The Residents' Bad Day on the Midway
The Cryptic Corporation, The Residents, Jim Ludtke

The Residents are a band that mixes
music with masquerade and bizarre
routines, so it comes as no suprise that
they are fond of the circus. Their first
CD–ROM, The Residents' Freak Show,
was a browsable collection of human
(and a few inhuman) misfits on display in
a circus tent. Bad Day on the Midway
enlarges this environment to a
nocturnal amusement park,
inhabited by strange creatures like
Madam Mandrake, a fortune–telling lady
who guides visitors through this
Disneyland of the Damned and whose
booth on Midway serves as 'home' for the
CD–ROM. The unforgettable cast of
characters is involved in a bizarre murder
mystery, set in a **surrealistic**
3D carnival with an original soundtrack
by The Residents.

*The IRS man is one of the strange characters that guide us through Midway. Here
the strange contrast between foreground animation and the ingeniously rendered
backdrop of the Amusement park is at its strongest. The characters seem strange-
ly detached from their world, they are our guides but are also an inextricable part
of the eerie environment.*

29

Year of publication 1995 **Author** The Cryptic Corporation, The Residents, Jim Ludtke **Place of publication** Los Angeles, CA, USA **Publisher** Inscape

Copyright owners Inscape **Design company** Inscape, The Cryptic Corporation **Screen design** Jim Ludtke, Iain Lamb **Animation / graphics** Jim Ludtke

Sound design The Residents **Production** The Residents, Jim Ludtke, Sharon Ludtke, Iain Lamb **Editors** The Residents

Software used EI, MMMM, AAE, MMD, APS, AI **Platform** mac / mpc

The Residents have been through a multitude of genres – recorded music to performance art to music video to graphic novels and multimedia CD-ROM. Their Bad Day on The Midway is a unique **experience** combining compelling interactive story lines with exciting game-play in a 3D world like no other. It features probability-based variable character interaction and lightning-fast 3D navigation. Highlights include graphic novels and art designed by such noted contributors as David McKeon (Mr. Punch, Sandman) and Jamie Hewitt (Tank Girl).

The CD-ROM is structured like a game in which you have to find the answers to some mysteries and evade the **haunting** dangers that lurk behind the dramatically lit facades of the attractions on 'Midway'. Mouse-navigating through this eerie environment, you will meet animated characters that look like degenerate relatives of the Thunderbird family and gradually discover their secrets.

The navigation through the park's space can be slow and hesitating. One has the time to examine each image and take a close look in every corner by clicking on hot spots. Here we quickly check out Lottie's fortune-telling booth before we keep the mouse button pressed to embark on a roller coaster-like ride into the park. The possibility of changing the tempo of the movement at will in any of the scenes is a great improvement over Freak Show, where only slow navigation was possible. The very exciting fast mode is achieved by a technique called pixel doubling; the screen's resolution is temporarily reduced to allow for great speed of movement.

Bad Day on the Midway is designed as an adult, comic–book amusement park, with as much glowing colours as your screen can handle. There is a touch of 'camp' in this deliberately kitschy colour range; the same goes for the grotesqueness of the characters and the setting. The CD–ROM is actually a cartoon movie that consists of one extended ride along a **meandering** path through the park, entering and leaving different attractions and mysterious corners, shifting from extreme wide–angle to close–up peeping and back again. Viewers control the projector, not the camera, as they wander through this slightly over–the–top, nightmarish decor. It is a cosy nightmare; you can sit back and relax while pondering the question: Can you survive The Residents' Bad Day on the Midway?

MAX BRUINSMA

Otto, Ted and Timmy are three more of the twenty–four amazingly different and rich characters Ludtke created for Bad Day. The animated characters speak with the recorded voices of actors as in Freak Show. What gives them their strong quality is a technique reminiscent of media-artist Tony Oursler's pillow projection works. The bodies and facial structure of the protagonists are computer rendered but the textures and facial expressions are video images of actors' faces, mapped on the heads of the puppets. The sometimes very loose alignment of the video with the puppets' heads is caused by the fact that the volume of the heads doesn't change shape in sync with the changes in expression and the movement of speaking. This a-synchronicity adds an extra alienating touch to the action that can hit you right in the stomach.

Now his long-awaited dream comes true.

Bio•morph Encyclopedia Muybridge
Nobuhiro Shibayama

A lavish 4D credit logo page sets the tone for a sumptuous disk.

The logo page is followed by a French Page offering a choice between the Japanese and English version of the CD–ROM.

Why would anyone build a car that looked like a slight improvement on the model T Ford with a state–of–the–art, computer-controlled motor concealed under the hood? At first glance, it would seem that Nobuhiro Shibayama has been doing just that. The Bio•morph Encyclopedia is a reworking of some of Muybridge's famous photographic **sequences** of moving men, women and animals made at the end of the nineteenth century. Shibayama 'animated' the original sequences by morphing the twelve stages of each sequence into each other, suggesting a seamless movement.

The introduction sequence to the actual Bio•Morph Encyclopedia suggests the endless space of a Borges–like library where history is omni present.

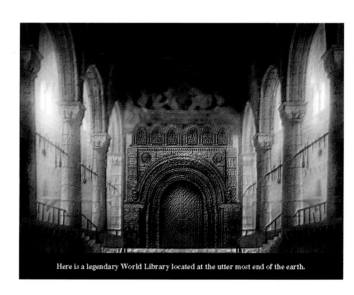

Here is a legendary World Library located at the utter most end of the earth.

Year of publication 1994 **Author** Nobuhiro Shibayama **Place of publication** Tokyo, Japan **Publisher** 4D. **Copyright owners** Nobuhiro Shibayama

Design company 4D. **Screen design** Nobuhiro Shibayama **Animation / graphics** Nobuhiro Shibayama, Tetsu Mukojima, Takumi Takahashi

Interaction design Nobuhiro Shibayama **Sound design** Kenichi Sato **Production** 4D. **Editors** 4D. **Software used** MMD, P, GM, APS **Platform** mac

Bio•morph Encyclopedia endeavours to fill in the gaps between the moments that Muybridge captured with his battery of cameras. However, the movies that result from this procedure are far from seamless. In effect, the morphed sequences accentuate the gaps more than they succeed in concealing them. Bio•morph Encyclopedia is about the **impossibility** of capturing time, a sensory condition that is graphical-ly depicted in the chimerically distorted lines that accompany the morphing pro-cess. As one stage of a sequence flows into another, the rigidly straight grid against which Muybridge photographed his models in motion twists and deforms, on the verge of dissolving, before - temporari-ly - reforming itself.

These contorted lines take on a typographic quality as signs of manipulation and symbols of our **confused** experience of time. Apart from 'updating' Muybridge's plates technically, Shibayama stresses the historic quality and the old-ness of the images by his manipulations and the formal context in which he presents them. The work is shown as an old book with lavish Victorian decorations and quasi-medieval miniatures. The introduction places it in a Borges-like library, suggesting a mysterious provenance from an endless space where history is ever-present. This enigmatic atmosphere is enhanced by devices like the hidden doors, animated pictograms that indicate the opening and closing of the Bio•morph movie sections.

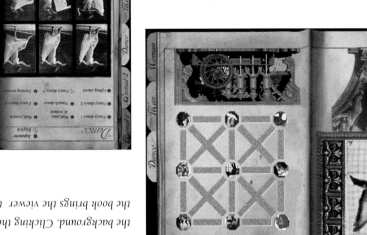

Catalogue page, showing twelve Muybridge plates from which a Bio•Morph Movie will be made. Clicking the captions in the upper right-hand area will give data on the original images.

Specification page from the Animals 2 chapter, showing an intermediate frame of the pigeon animation. Note the waveform distortion of the straight grid in the background. Clicking the tabs in the margins of the book brings the viewer to other chapters.

Before accessing the actual Encyclopedia, there is a bio-graphical section on Muybridge's life.

One day, a chief librarian of this library received a request from a photographer named Muybridge in the 19th century.

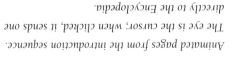

...that this library is a mysterious place ...re and after death, all existing in one space.

Animated pages from the introduction sequence. The eye is the cursor; when clicked, it sends one directly to the Encyclopedia.

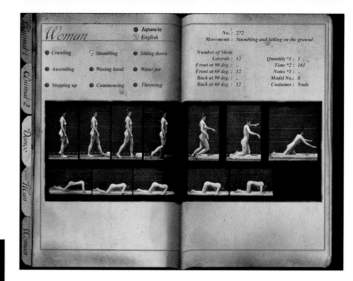

In a biographical section, Muybridge tells his own history in a distorted voice that seems to come from beyond the grave — a form of audio-typography that matches the old book metaphor of the visual design used throughout the disc, from the **heavy leather** cover to the 'calligraphed' captions.

Besides this historicising surface, the CD–ROM offers the very modern possibility of combining different animated sequences to form a personal Bio•morph movie in which different animals, men and women morph into each other. In the gaps between the original images a new breed of hybrid creatures appears, a mixture of myth and science fiction.

MAX BRUINSMA

From the Memory pole (right), at the end of the disk, the user can view the Bio•Morph Movies they have interactively generated in each chapter. When clicked, they appear in the window left.

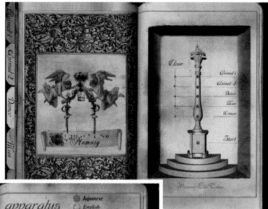

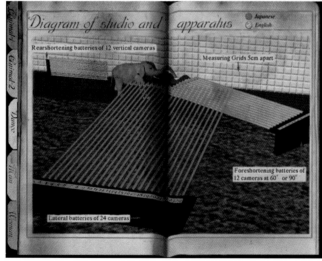

A schematic view of the studio set–up Muybridge used in capturing his moving subjects.

35

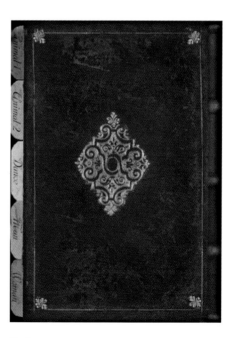

End page.

uitleg

House / Huis / Joost Grootens

Young Dutch artist and designer Joost Grootens designed a house on the shore, on the constantly shifting **borderline** between land and sea. The house will become an island as the sea pushes back the land. It would seem natural that this house built on sand exists only in its architect's imagination.

The house is more of a mindscape than 'real' architecture. Its outlines are roughly drawn to give an impression of what might be a site. It is built of associations of mobility and permanence, security and ambivalence, formalised in a collection of sketches, photos, notes and quotes from poetry and other sources. It is there and not there, depending on how you look at it. Grootens illustrates the impossibility of **certainty** in these matters with the one piece of 'furniture' his house contains: a stuffed rhinoceros – an allusion to Ludwig Wittgenstein's refusal to admit to Bertrand Russell that the obvious absence of this massive animal in the classroom in which they were lecturing was proven.

First page of the Story section. Clicking the numbers produces a sentence or animation sample. Clicking the animation activates the short sequence of images and texts.

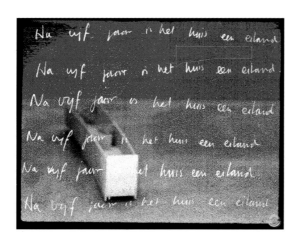

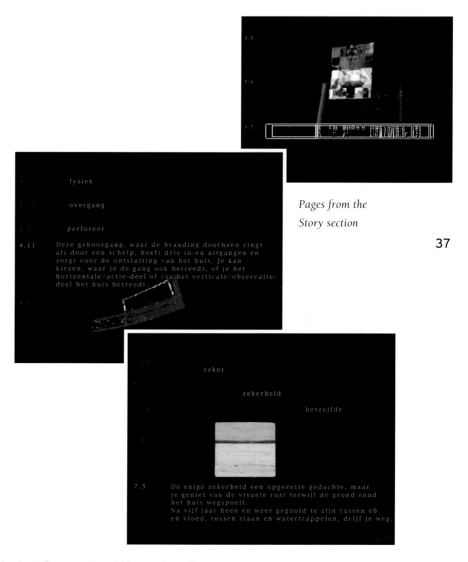

Pages from the Story section

37

Year of publication 1995 Author Joost Grootens Place of publication Amsterdam, Netherlands Publisher Joost Grootens Copyright owner Joost Grootens

Design company J005T6R00T3N5 Screen design Joost Grootens Animation / graphics Joost Grootens Interaction design Joost Grootens Sound design Joost Grootens

Production Joost Grootens Editor Joost Grootens Contributor Joost Grootens Software used MMD Platform mac

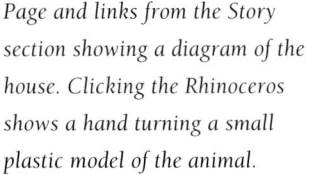

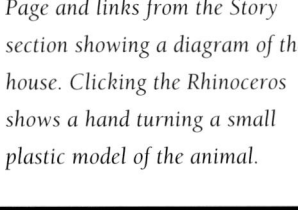

Page and links from the Story section showing a diagram of the house. Clicking the Rhinoceros shows a hand turning a small plastic model of the animal.

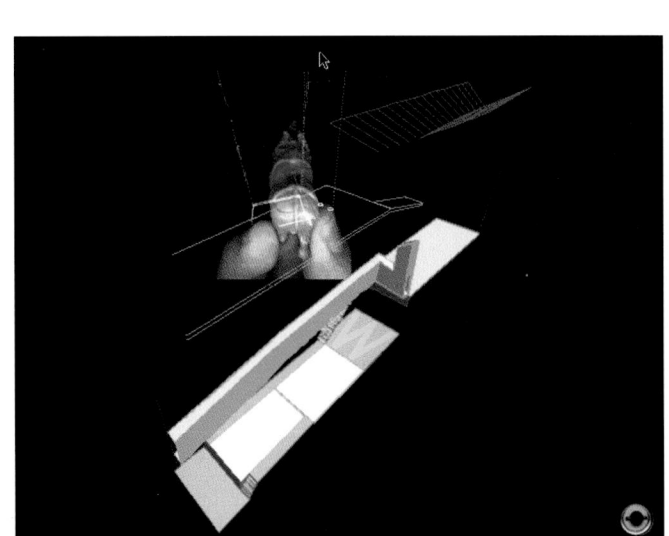

Grootens offers three interfaces with the material he collected: the Story, the Sentence and the Word. The second and third are opposites of random access and systematic reference, aptly metaphorized as a 'fruit machine' and a 'directory/folder' structure. The fruit machine is a window with tumbling images and words that stop at a click, giving one of twenty–seven sentences and a still image. When clicked again it gives a short animation. The folder structure gives clickable access to the complete library of discrete items on the CD–ROM. The main difference between the two is **illusory:** the random-ness of the Sentence is as structured as the system behind the Word is poetically irra-tional. The first interface, the Story, is a narrative organised in the same way as Wittgenstein's Tractatus. It is a (simple) hypertext structure that allows you to follow Grootens' associations and view the corresponding image material. House is in essence a poetic project that plays with the (im)possibilities of rationally structuring associations.

Links showing sections of the house and associations with sites and building.

The Sentence section is a fruit machine that randomly combines three layers of tumbling images and words. It stops at a click. Clicking the clover sign shows a short animation or text.

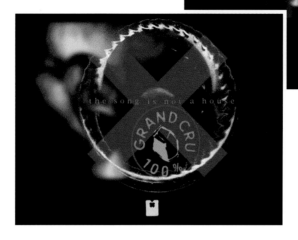

The graphic design of the three interfaces – in its subtle play with the graphical and typographical clichés of linear narrative, **random browsing** and systematic reference – suggests three fundamentally different bodies of information, whereas all three 'environments' are made of the same material; a house of associations, built on sand.

MAX BRUINSMA

Images from the Sentence section. The same visual material is used in the other sections. Only the context and access are different.

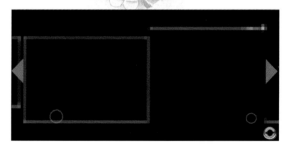

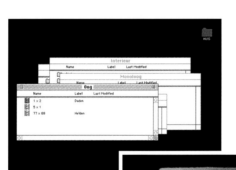

The third section – Word – uses a folder structure to organize the material. Clicking a filmstrip logo activates an animation.

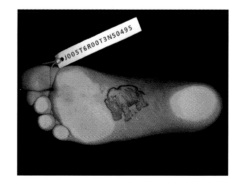

'Signature' of the maker of House.

the front entrance
garden

The Foundation Marguerite and Aimé Maeght: a Stroll in Twentieth Century Art

Bastide Bastide & Bastide

The Maeght Collection is housed in a museum in the south of France, surrounded by a sculpture garden and a 'labyrinth' with works by Spanish artist Juan Miró. The CD–ROM provides for different ways of accessing the artworks on show: walking around the premises, **jumping** like a bee from one work to the other and browsing through the reference library. In addition, there is a biographical section that gives an insight into the lives of Marguerite and Aimé Maeght, the collectors that brought together this amazingly rich overview of the now classic art of the first half of this century.

The richness of the collection is matched by the variety of possibilities to access the information. With the (Quicktime) walk through the collection as basis, you can step out at any point to get a better view of a work, look up its data, jump to a biography and catalogue of the artist or find out about its art historical context or its place in the collection. Hyperlinks provide connections to related artists and the lives of the collectors.

Title page

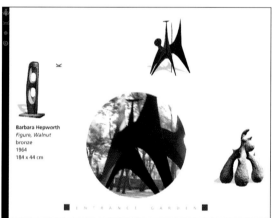

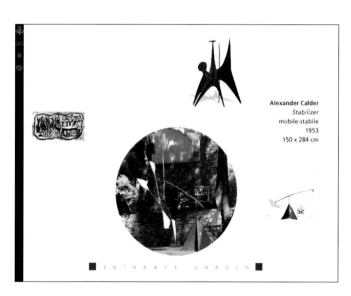

In the circle, a Quicktime movie shows a Stroll through the sculpture garden. When the camera passes a work, it appears in the margin. Moving the cursor over it produces information about the work.

41

Year of publication 1995 Author Bastide Bastide & Bastide Place of publication Paris, France Publisher Matra Hachette Multimédia, Maeght Éditeur

Copyright owners Matra Hachette Multimédia, Maeght Éditeur Awards International EMMA Award Winner '95 Design company Bastide Bastide & Bastide Screen design Bastide Bastide & Bastide Animation / graphics Bastide Bastide & Bastide Interaction design Bastide Bastide & Bastide Sound design Bastide Bastide & Bastide Production Matra Hachette Multimédia, Maeght Éditeur

Editors Matra Hachette Multimédia, Maeght Éditeur Contributors Pascale Bastide, Patric Pleutin, Étienne Auger, Marylène Lérault, Léticia Zitouni, Pascale Courtois, P. Hébrard, B.P. Molin, F. Tolédano Platform mac / mpc

The extended apparatus of the inter-face has been modestly disguised as small signets in the margin: a bee to 'jump' from one work to the other, a sign to click to the plan of the museum, a **spiral** to browse through the biography of the Maeghts. Clicking the white arch in the margin brings you back to where you left the Walk. It is like strolling through the collection with a catalogue in your hands; you stop and watch and leaf through the pages and go on again. 'Audio–typography' enhances the feel of walking through the park and the museum. Outside, the warm **summer** sound of crickets pre-vails; inside, one hears the shuffling feet and the soft murmur of invisible visitors.

Nicolas de Stael
Nude Study
charcoal on paper
1955
150 × 100 cm

A page from the Stroll through the cloister section.

The interactive map gives an overview of the prem-ises and accesses the different areas of the Foundation. Note information on the history of the Foundation in left–hand margin.

THE GIACOMETTI COURTYARD
MIRO'S LABYRINTH
THE TOWN HALL WING
BRAQUE'S POOL
THE CLOISTER
CHAPEL ST BERNARD
ENTRANCE GARDEN

The Foundation's key figures
Exhibitions 1964 · 1971 · 1975 · 1979 · 1984 · 1988
The foundation's night 1965 · 1967 · 1969 · 1970

• Surface area of the land :
10,540 m2.
• Surface area of the exhibition
rooms: 860 m2.
• Surface area of the Giacometti
Courtyard : 450 m2.
• Number of visitors since the
Foundation's opening:
3 720,000 including 109,690 for the
Matisse exhibition in 1973.
119,000 for the Chagall exhibition in
1984
146,400 for 'L'Œuvre Ultime' in
1989.
• Number of exhibitions held at the
Foundation:
89 from April 1966 to October 1994.

Clicking the work in the margin accesses a Catalogue and Biography.

The term denotes
the stabilizers
placed at the rear
of arrows and
airplanes.

The dance of the world

A **mobile** is a combination of movements and rhythms, a kind of choreography that comes into relation with other types of movements and rhythms.

"... they are at the same time poetic technical, almost mathematical combinations, and the tangible symbol of Nature, that great vague Nature that squanders pollen and makes a thousand butterflies suddenly take wing."

Jean-Paul Sartre
French philosopher,
writer and critic,
1905–1980.

This CD–ROM is a very complete and carefully designed introduction to the Maeght Collection. Typographically, it could be described in terms of the 'page metaphor': a lay–out that neatly arranges the information, visually **linking** image and text and providing each 'chapter' with its own distinct graphic character. But they are interactive pages, and they move — part of this Catalogue turns its own pages. As the movie passes one work after another, pictures accompanied by their Catalogue descriptions pop up around the circular screen.

MAX BRUINSMA

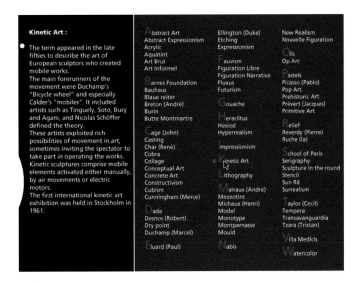

Hyperlinked register page. The text of the triggered item appears in the left–hand margin.

Three phases in browsing from the Stroll through the Miró Labyrinth via the Bee–option, which displays the complete range of works corresponding to the Catalogue selection.

Three phases in browsing the biographical section of founders Aimé and Marguerite Maeght. The first page gives an overview. When clicked, the photos access three or four pages of information with Quicktime movies in the margin. Clicking the Lizard pictogram starts an audio registration of interview clips.

43

Puppet Motel / Laurie Anderson

Is Time long, or is it wide...?

There could hardly be an artist better suited to venture into the CD–ROM medium than multimedia artist and performer Laurie Anderson. Commenting on popular culture in general and American culture in particular, she combines text, video, electronic and pop music into multi–layered performances. However, her strength has always been in telling **stories.** While her stage show performances gathered ever–larger audiences, they always retained a very intimate quality. A quality very well suited to CD–ROM.

Like in many other CD–ROMs, Laurie Anderson and designer Hsin–Chien Huang use a spatial, architectural metaphor, the Puppet Motel. The title – taken from one of her songs – refers to **virtual life** in MOO's and explains the MOO–like layout of the Motel. A time dimension is added as well, exploring a spatial notion of time — or is it a temporal notion of space? Upon entering you find yourself in a dark 'corridor of time' – two revolving clocks indicate an indeterminable moment in time.

Puppet Motel's main navigation channel, a corridor in time and space. The icons appearing on the left–hand wall will take you to the Icerink, the Music room and the TV room.

45

Year of publication 1995 **Author** Laurie Anderson **Place of publication** New York, USA **Publisher** The Voyager Company **Copyright owners** The Voyager Company, Canal Street Communications, Inc.

Screen design Hsin-Chien Huang **Animation / graphics** Hsin-Chien Huang, Laurie Anderson **Sound design** Laurie Anderson, Mark Coniglio **Production** Elizabeth Scarborough, Philippe Stessel, Lisa Pedicini

Editors Elizabeth Scarborough, Reid Sherline, David Ekrem, Rebekka Linton, Anderson Tepper **Additional Programmers** Chi-Kang Peng, John Thompson, Colin Holgate

Technical Director Morgan Holly **Audio Post Production** Sean Anderson, Rex C. Arthur, Mark C. Brems, Chris Burke **Production Manager** Lissa Cobetto **Platform** mac

The icerink transforms the cursor into a skating shoe, allowing 3D movement, so you can explore the depth as well as the width and height of the screen.

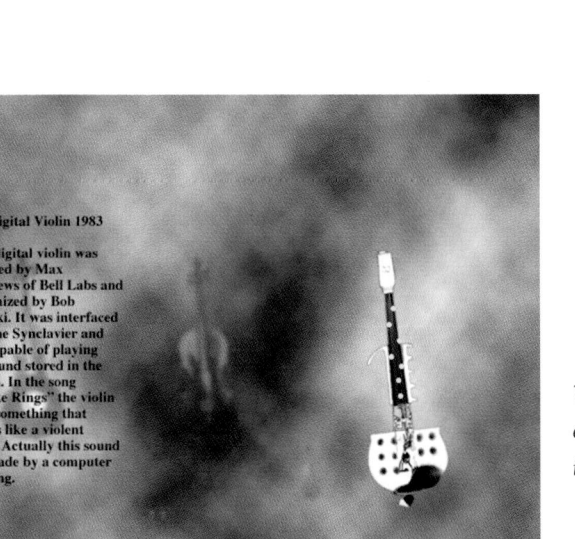

The Digital Violin 1983

The digital violin was designed by Max Matthews of Bell Labs and customized by Bob Bielecki. It was interfaced with the Synclavier and was capable of playing any sound stored in the system. In the song "Smoke Rings" the violin plays something that sounds like a violent storm. Actually this sound was made by a computer crashing.

The Musicroom features three e–violins, sound samples and information about the instruments.

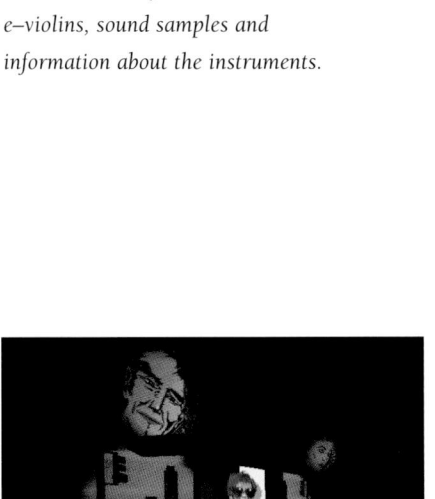

Icons appear while moving through the corridor, referring to some thirty (or more) rooms. There is a waiting room, a writing room with typewriter, a music room allowing you to bow Laurie's e–violins, a **skating** rink, a stage and a phone room that allows you to connect to the Net and download material from the related site on the World Wide Web.

Puppet Motel is beautifully designed, breathing the suspenseful atmosphere of a David Lynch movie, full of hidden surprises. Navigation is partly determined by the icons, appearing and disappearing like **ghostly** visions, but also by hidden buttons that require inquisitive actions by the user/guest.

The ouija board will answer any of your questions, or will it?

The stage features a collection of stories, performances and links to other rooms. The puppet lip–syncs Puppet Motel and Laurie talks about her violin. The performances are triggered by clicking the 'X's on the floor.

The phone room is the Puppet Motel's outside line, where you can connect to the Voyager web site to download updated information.

The writing room is designed like a detective's office from a film noir. A piece of paper appears as one explores the room. Typing on your keyboard causes an old typewriter on screen to type several prepared texts.

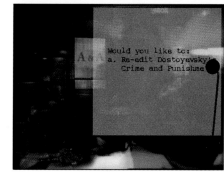

Puppet Motel contains several fascinating interface solutions, involving dragging and dropping objects or 'plugging and unplugging' appliances. In some rooms, the cursor is **transformed** into a three-dimensional object that allows you to move in all three axial directions. In another room, the cursor directs a ray of light coming through a window. Travelling across the darkened room, the light animates the objects it hits to tell their stories.

Exploring Puppet Motel produces a rich, layered collage of stories, images and music very true to the nature of Laurie Anderson's work. It seems that she has found the medium that allows her to use the **full swing** of multimedia to tell her story with great intimacy.

GEERT J. STRENGHOLT

The attic is a collection of objects referring to most of the other rooms.

47

Taking a cutting from the rack and dropping it on the editing table allows you to play short pieces of animation or film. To leave the cutting room, you take the cutting from the waste basket and play it to get the escape icon on screen.

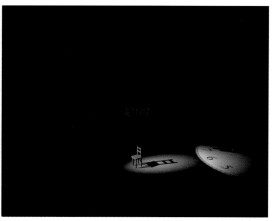

The waiting room... time revolves around a single chair, illuminating several clocks.

ScruTiny In The Great Round
Tennessee Rice Dixon, Jim Gasperini

Some movies defy description. When asked: What was it about?, you answer: I have no idea, but it looked great! ScruTiny could be best described in **roughly** the same way: as an (interactive) movie that leaves you with a clear understanding of its beauty without being able to pinpoint its contents.

In essence, ScruTiny is a linear structure of heavily symbolic images that grow out of each other, appearing from the background and then vanishing. There is no rigid narrative order, but the images are closely knit together — with the inescapable logic of dreams. The imagery is also of the stuff that **dreams** are made of: mythical archetypes of conception and birth, man and woman, God and Creation.

The title page sequence offers a short animation that summarises the hallucinatory atmosphere of the CD–ROM, showing creatures that morph into one another. Here, a fish swims through this fairy–tale wood.

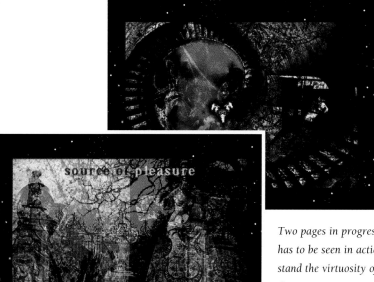

Two pages in progress — this is a CD–ROM that has to be seen in action to appreciate and understand the virtuosity of the morphing sequences and the screen transitions fully.

49

Year of publication 1995 **Author** Tennessee Rice Dixon, Jim Gasperini **Place of publication** Santa Monica, CA, USA **Publisher** Calliope Media **Copyright owners** ScruTiny Associates **Awards** New Voices New Visions '94 **Design company** ScruTiny Associates **Screen design** Tennessee Rice Dixon, Jim Gasperini **Animation / graphics design** Tennessee Rice Dixon, Jim Gasperini **Interaction design** Tennessee Rice Dixon, Jim Gasperini **Sound design** Charlie Morrow, Jim Gasperini, Jeff Rabb, Tennessee Rice Dixon **Production** Tennessee Rice Dixon, Jim Gasperini, Charlie Morrow, Jeff Rabb **Editors** Tennessee Rice Dixon, Jim Gasperini **Contributors** Bill Gasperini, Kim Lyons, Sabina Elustan, Phillip Alego Braun **Software used** MMD, AAE, GM, APS, PT, MMS **Platform** mac / mpc

Twenty-two 'pages' each conceal a number of clickable spots that trigger short animations, morphed sequences, and texts from the global library of symbols: the Bible, the Koran, the Bhagavad–Gita, the Tao, the Tibetan Book of the Dead and William Blake's poetry. The graphic design of the interface is in harmony with this **mystic atmosphere:** hybrids of man and bird point to previous and following pages, hotspots light up as a moon or a sun (the contents of the disc have been divided into a night and a day section) and the typography emulates calligraphy–on–parchment, evoking ancient manuscripts. One can leaf through this book in a non–linear way, but the option of 'continuous movement' that plays all the material on the CD–ROM in a fixed order suggests that the disc is actually more an animated book than an interactive event.

One of twelve sunside main pages. Moving the cursor over the screen reveals 'hot spots' where the sun or the moon lights up. Clicking the lady at the vat will start an animation compiled of very disparate material.

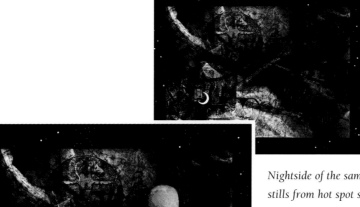

Typography plays a modest role here. The CD–ROM is mainly a virtuoso play with images. Layer upon layer, these images add up to a dark forest from which shady creatures **materialise** and into which they dissolve again. Tumbling chromosomes and other microscopic structures dance around or merge with astrological charts, pictures of seeds and plants, religious sculptures, pages and illustrations from age–old books, photographs and Quicktime movies of running horses.

This alchemy of images from very disparate sources is held together by a consistent use of texture and colour (grainy and subdued) and of sound. Mysterious noises from the rain forests of our collective unconsciousness combine with distant piano chords, **humming** choirs and solemnly quoted lines from the Wise to evoke an image of revealed truth — not to be understood but to be thankfully accepted.

MAX BRUINSMA

Nightside of the same main page with two stills from hot spot sequences.

51

Floating kernel will morph into a new–born baby, that will come down in a new page...

Education

An Anecdoted Archive from The Cold War,
George Legrady, 1994

In education, the best multimedia is: going there, being there. Learning by doing — it is the metaphor of the Grand Tour, where you actively follow the tracks of the culture you were born into, reading and hearing the stories in the contexts in which they were first told. And having your own private Virgil to guide you. Books can hardly do what this teacher can: answer your questions and follow associations into other directions, thus teaching you to connect what seemed unconnected.

A CD–ROM is better than a book in this respect. It is a replayable Grand Tour. The designer of this virtual *tour d'horizon* formally links the episodes, reminding the student at all points of where they have come from and where they are going. A sign, an image, a sound activates the memory — it has to act in order to experience — and each screen reminds the viewer of the fact that all is connected, once remembered.

Graphic design in educational publications in multimedia has greater freedom of form than in print publications — in print, the internal structure of the material and the graphic representation of it largely coincide. This is not the case in multimedia. All kinds of formal connections between the information that must be explicit in print can hide behind a click on a CD–ROM. Here, the interactions between the different layers of information have to be actively experienced instead of doggedly memorised. Graphic design for educational multimedia is an active force in helping the student experience the information — it brings it to life.

Each screen is a phase in a goal–oriented process. The connections between texts, images and reference material, the visualisation of hyperlinks, the hierarchies in different layers of information that are invisible at first sight, all have to be designed in such a way that they stimulate and help the student to follow the narrative, because in most cases the CD–ROM is structured as a narrative, a story that is told not in a literary, linear way, but in the way good storytellers relate their adventures: by raising and lowering their voice, by their gestures and facial expression, by jumping from anecdote to detail to general context. They adjust their story to the ears and eyes of their listeners. As the 'voice' of the teacher, the designer tries to give form to these sensory aspects of learning, helping the viewers to experience and memorise the relationships between details, structure and whole. The design leaves room for interaction, but rarely stimulates random browsing. This makes way for the educated guess.

MAX BRUINSMA

53

Whenever it got quiet, my mothe would come out of the cellar. At some point she met a young German soldier posted in the entrance way. At a later time she came out and found him leaning over, his body frozen in rigor mortis, photos of his family and girl friend fallen on the ground.

An Anecdoted Archive From the Cold War
George Legrady

George Legrady contrasts his personal archive and narrative of his family leaving Hungary with the official narrative of the state of Hungary from the same period. He calls his An Anecdoted Archive a **hybrid synthesis** between two points of origin in terms of storytelling as a way to understand that moment of crisis.

The disk uses the floor plan of the Worker's Movement Museum in Budapest to situate a series of stories, both personal and official. The interface indeed has the formal look of a museum display device, containing an 'archive' with highly entertaining references. There is the story of the purchase and nationalisation of his grandfather's house, which became a factory, then a workers' vacation home, before being re–privatized; a series of banknotes trace the major shifts Hungary has experienced through foreign intervention since 1849. Legrady charts his father's **musical** career with radio broadcasts, news clippings and photos.

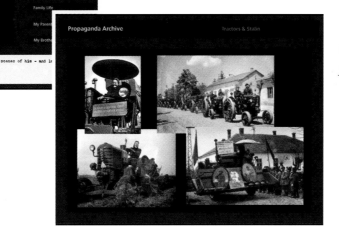

Possession of a Pathé Baby cinecamera produced a stock of family stories between 1948 and their flight in 1956.

Smiling for Uncle Joe; the happy farmers of the Propaganda Archive.

The Museum's floor plan is the introductory interface, with roll–over menu choice (Stories) activated.

The interface and disk contents offer a concrete realisation of philosophical concepts of knowledge and objects.

Year of publication 1994 Author George Legrady Place of publication San Francisco, USA Publisher George Legrady

Copyright owners George Legrady Awards New Voices, New Visions, Voyager, Interval Research '95 Design company HyperReal Media Productions Screen design Andrea Schwartz

Interaction design George Legrady, Rosemary Comella Production Hyper Real, Rosemary Comella Platform mac

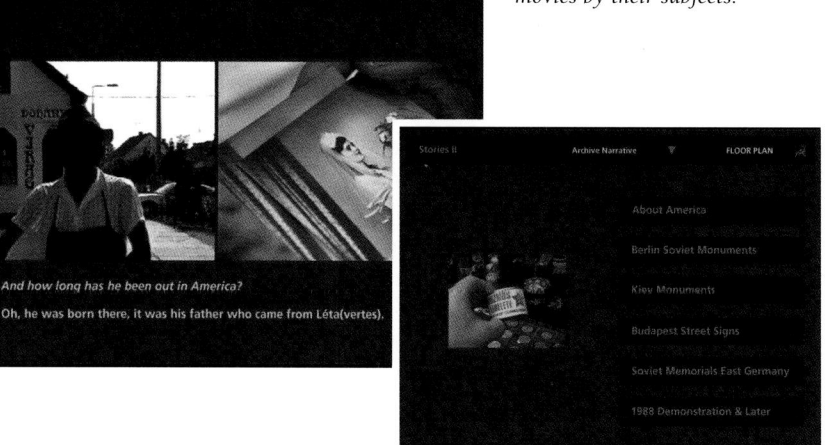

Some of the Stories are told in QuickTime movies by their subjects.

In 1988 (left), the first anti–Communist demonstrations in Hungary were captured on video by Legrady. Three years later, it was all over, bar the merchandising.

The minimal interface is refreshingly transparent to use. Left, a tin of the last breath of Communism.

Scanned personal **memorabilia** such as pressed flowers, bus cards and personal documents rub shoulders with book and LP covers, recordings of dissident speeches and elderly family members, Pathé Baby home movies and video QuickTime clips. Contrasted with the Propaganda Archive of the museum (heroic songs and movie reel clips of happy farmers), it is a showcase of how CD–ROMS allow mundane material to be re–woven in new contexts. In Border Crossings, Legrady compares his experiences crossing from Hungary to Canada, Canada to the US and, later, Austria to Hungary, showing that officialdom the world over is often crass, stupid and vindictive.

The day the Russians moved in: newspapers around the world differed in their response. Here, Pravda leads with British aggression in Egypt...

...while others focus on the quashed Budapest uprising.

By the late eighties, Budapest was already just another exotic location for magazines like Vogue. Legrady nicely juxtaposes images from East and West, past and present, to illustrate the sometimes bizarre contradictions of imagery.

The interface is unobtrusive and deliberately conservative; this is definitely a disk of content and not a critique of digital style. The viewer is **forced** to search and interact — otherwise it is just a simple interface staring back. Other features, such as roll–over translations of official documents and their stamps, give a clean, easy feel to the interface.

An Anecdoted Archive binds the empathic power of the visual with the contemplative quietude of a book. In the 40–60 minutes it takes to access most of the material on the disc, the user's perspective on this period of history is stimulated in a way impossible with TV or books. Here, An Anecdoted Archive manifests its special educational value, in which personal history triggers a broader, national history.

Legrady notes that in producing the title, his perspective on the era has also crystallised. An Anecdoted Archive is a **significant signpost** to the sort of artefact we can hope for if the dream of mass multimedia literacy comes about.

JULES MARSHALL

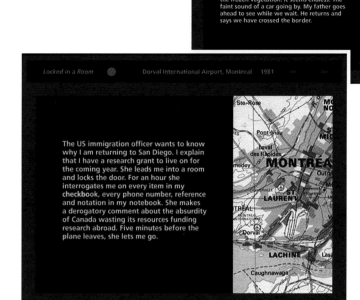

Border crossings: an émigré is doomed to eternal harassment, petty and not so petty, wherever he goes.

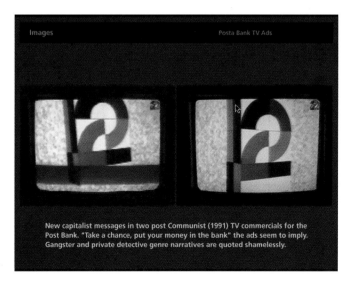

Legrady turns his California–honed ad deconstruction skills on Budapest's nascent advertising industry.

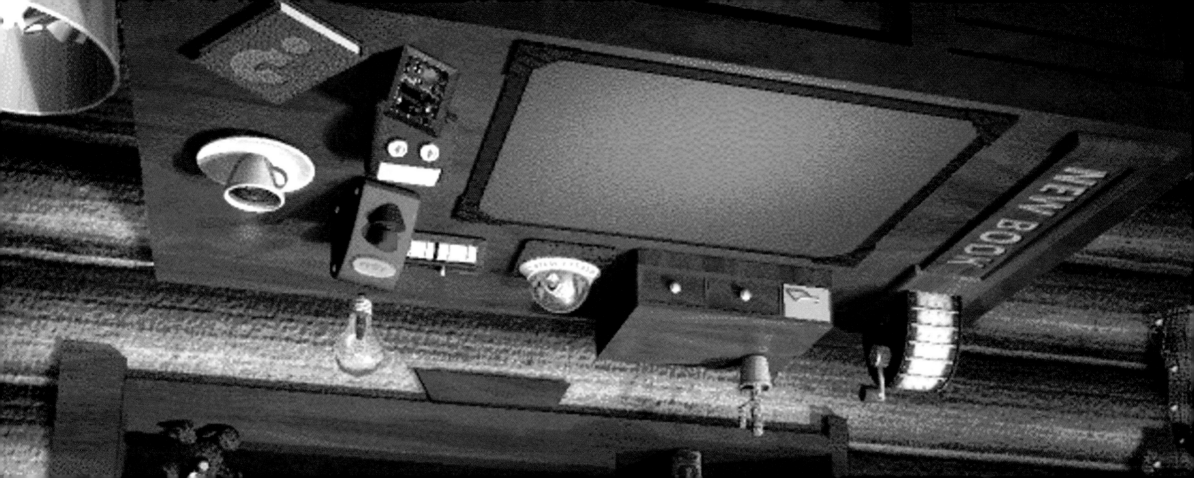

Echo Lake / Delrina Corporation

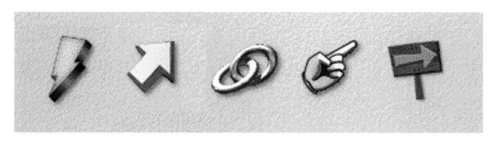

Echo Lake is a tool for writing. The program is designed for anyone who feels the urge to record his memoirs. It can be an inspiring family experience to put all the material brought back from a holiday into this **multimedia diary.** The software creates a virtual space which guides and nudges the prospective author with a variety of hints, distractions and associations.

The basic application is not particularly new. It is a multimedia word processor with a graphic interface. The innovative aspect however is that the interface develops a consistent metaphor which seduces the user to transport himself to the virtual space of Echo Lake. The lake in question is located somewhere in the wilderness surrounded by mountains and pine trees.

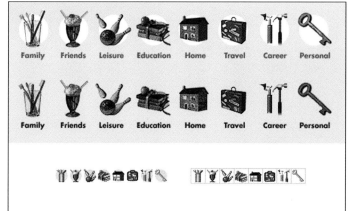

The Icons can be cut and pasted individually to embellish the layout . They have both a functional and decorative purpose.

Year of publication 1995 **Author** Delrina Corporation **Place of publication** Toronto, Ontario, Canada **Publisher** Delrina Corporation **Copyright owners** Delrina (Wyoming) Limited Liability Company **Awards** Byte Best of Comdex '95: Finalist - Best Multimedia Product, New MediaInvision Awards '95: Finalist, Electronic Link Awards '95: Best Interface Design, International Digital Media Awards '95: Finalist, Demo '95: Premiere Product **Design company** Delrina Corporation **Screen design** Greg Long, Kevin Steele, Jeremy Cooke **Animation / graphics** Greg Long, Kevin Steele, Jeremy Cooke **Interaction design** Greg Long, Kevin Steele, Jeremy Cooke **Sound design** Greg Long, Kevin Steele, Jeremy Cooke **Production** Delrina Corporation **Editors** Delrina Corporation**Contributors** Chris Gudgeon, Sandra Bornn, Karl Borst **Software developers** Harry Snyder, Colin Miller, Scott Northmore, Skip Lamb, Steve Stedman, Mike Hamoaka, Gordon Barnes, John Kuhlman, Liwei Li, Cherian Zachariah **Platform** mac / mpc

Product packaging.

This is the opening Splash Screen that appears when the program boots up. It establishes the atmosphere of the 'cabin'. The menu shows how multiple 'authors' can be named to use the program.

The Book Cover where new books are named, dated, and other options are chosen.

60

Naturally the perfect environment for children to play in and for adults to put their minds off their daily worries. One lives in a cabin at the edge of a lake and writes at a desk near the window, occasionally gazing out in search of passing eagles while taking a coffee break.

The interface is designed to keep up this **homey illusion.** For instance, opening a document is accomplished by pulling the appropriate journal from the shelf, and the application is quit by putting on a logger's jacket hanging in the corner of the room. One interesting feature is an idea machine called The Inspirator which attempts to get the author past 'writer's block'. This is a scrapbook of popular culture since the forties which hopefully jars memories to be recorded.

There are built–in Record features within Echo Lake. Sound clips can be created (with 10–1 compression) while new stories are written.

Another example of a Story Page created in Echo Lake.

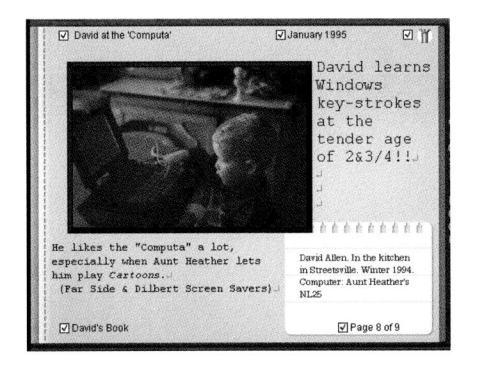

The chapters of each book are organised by subject on this elegant Tree Ring interface. Choose one of the red balls to open a chapter.

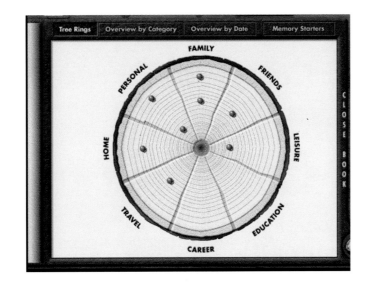

Aside from its simple beauty, the interface helps provide a sense of security and intimacy which may help some potential authors to make those grey cells waggle. This 'warm nest', interface can be contrasted to the interface of Word for Windows with its sharp lines and **metallic textures** which seems to embody futuristic clichés from science fiction films.

An obvious danger of such a homey metaphorical interface is that of another stylistic stereotype. The designer seems to have searched his subconscious for nostalgic images, and integrated these into a virtual space for others to make use of. Consequently, this space vaguely evokes an old Leave it to Beaver episode. However, in this case, the intentional clichés are part of the charm of the writing environment.

On the whole, Echo Lake represents a very inventive approach to the use of **graphic images** to achieve the functional goals of a computer program. The cultural-ly–loaded visuals succeed in providing a sense of safety and calling up old memories, which blends both the aspects of design and function perfectly. For this reason, Echo Lake is an inter-esting and innovative use of the electronic medium.

GREG BALL

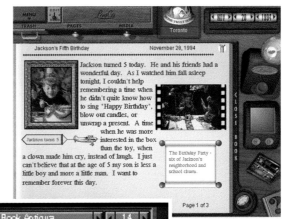

Close–up of the Media Drawer where users can easily import all types of graphics, photos, sounds, and video files. It also allows the user to add custom lines, tags and other fillable cards. The Bull represents OLE access.

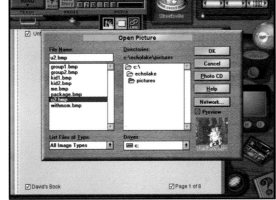

Click on the photo in the Media Drawer, and the Open Picture inter-face pops up. This allows you to find any compatible picture file on your hard drive, CD–ROM drive, or network drive, and import them to your Story Page. Also has Preview capability.

Improvisation Technologies
Volker Kuchelmeister, Christian Ziegler

There are basically two languages in which the complex movements of **modern dance** can be reproduced: graphic notation and video registration. In this CD–ROM (which documents the Improvisation Technologies project originally played from four hard discs), a combination of the two is used to demonstrate William Forsythe's dance method with almost scientific scrutiny.

The basis is Forsythe himself, demonstrating the movements from which he builds his repertoire. The 'lines' he uses or suggests with his body are made graphically visible while he tells the viewer what he's doing and why. This grammar of movements is then traced through rehearsals and performance of Forsythe's pieces by his group at the Frankfurt Ballet. Fragments of the performance can be viewed from four different camera perspectives.

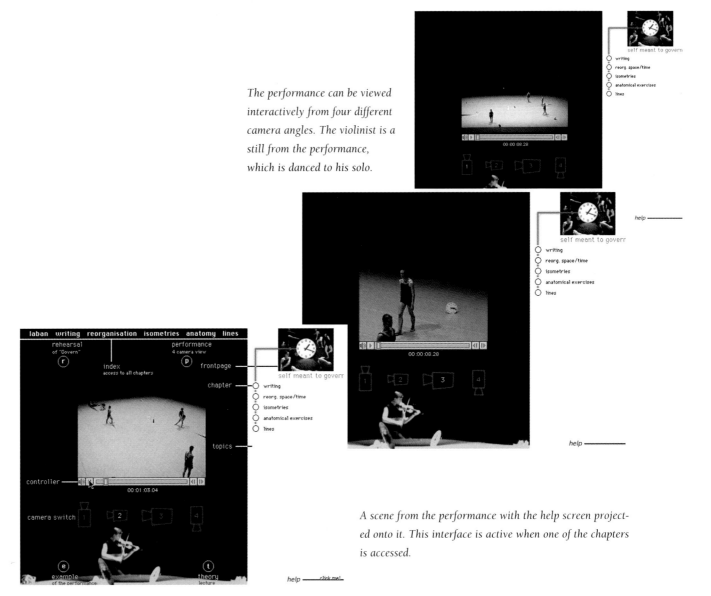

The performance can be viewed interactively from four different camera angles. The violinist is a still from the performance, which is danced to his solo.

63

A scene from the performance with the help screen projected onto it. This interface is active when one of the chapters is accessed.

Year of publication 1994 **Author** Volker Kuchelmeister, Christian Ziegler **Place of publication** Karlsruhe, Frankfurt, Germany **Publisher** ZKM (Center for Art and Media) Karlsruhe, Ballett Frankfurt
Copyright owners Volker Kuchelmeister, Christian Ziegler **Design company** Volker Kuchelmeister, Christian Ziegler **Screen design** Christian Ziegler **Animation / graphics** Christian Ziegler, Yvonne Mohr
Interaction design Volker Kuchelmeister, Christian Ziegler **Sound design** Ballet Frankfurt **Production** ZKM, Ballett Frankfurt **Software used** MMD, VG, APR, APS **Platform** harddisk

Around these demonstrations, rehearsals and performances, Forsythe has built an elaborate **theoretical structure** that can be accessed through an equally elaborate interface. Six main chapters on the theory are linked to each other and to the performance chapter over a front page. It is not an easy interface, but it is remarkably well laid-out, with a clear, stern typography that holds together an intricate web of links, references and functions. Most of the typographical interface is hidden when not in direct use, so it takes some study to find out its subtleties. It gives access to an interactive archive that enables dancers to study Forsythe's theory on their own and offers the audience a new way to get acquainted with the choreographies.

Scene from the rehearsal section.

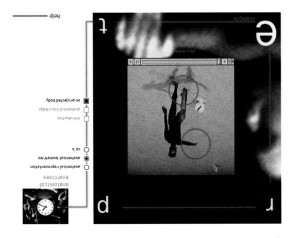

An example from the Self Meant to Govern performance demonstrates the use of 'anatomical isometries'. The isolated movement is repeated automatically, until another choice is made. Clicking the 'p' will show the same movement in the context of the performance. Clicking the 'r' will show the rehearsal of the movement.

Forsythe demonstrates a 'complex operation' called parallel shearing.

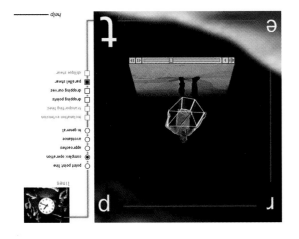

In the theoretical environment, Forsythe graphically demonstrates his catalogue of movements. Clicking on the 'e' links to an example of the same movement from the performance of Self Meant to Govern.

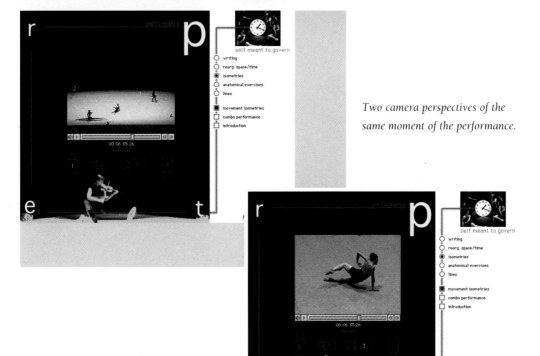

*Two camera perspectives of the
same moment of the performance.*

*A view of the performance of Forsythe's
Self Meant to Govern.*

This **digital dance school,** developed at the multi-media lab of the Zentrum für Kunst und Medientechnologie (ZKM) in Karlsruhe, is one of the CD–ROMs that effectively does away with the book and TV metaphors; there is no forced linearity in the proceedings. This in itself is an amazing feat, considering the theoretical nature of the disc. It is interactive in the sense that it provides ample opportunities for students of **Forsythe's method** to follow their own interests and make their own hierarchy in the material at hand.

MAX BRUINSMA

Credit page.

continue

Return to Daisy

POWER

She Loves It, She Loves It Not: Women and Technology
Christine Tamblyn

CD–ROM author Christine Tamblyn, says hello, introduces herself and the disk and then invites the user to enter by clicking on her mouth.

67

Women and Technology — do they love it or don't they? Some women might fantasise about a **future** in which robots equipped with all necessary appliances replace the human male and leave it at that. Others, like the author of this CD, explore and even build this future. On the opening screen of her CD–ROM, Christine Tamblyn presents herself in the flesh and grants the viewer access to her mind through a click on her invitingly wide–open mouth.

The petals of a daisy are the 'buttons' for interactivity. Browsing over this menu makes a word pop up in a wheel of fortune–like manner.

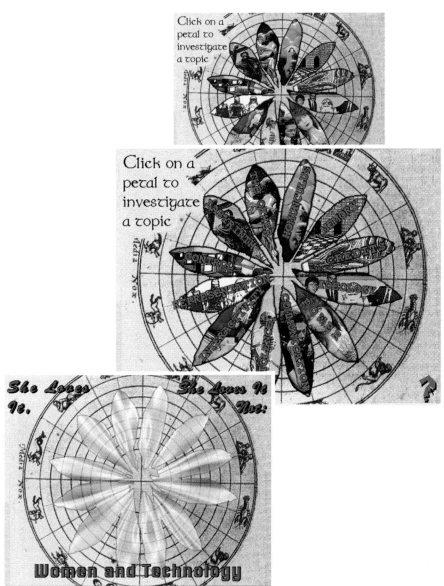

Year of publication 1993 **Author** Christine Tamblyn **Place of publication** San Francisco, USA **Publisher** Christine Tamblyn **Copyright owner** Christine Tamblyn
Awards New Voices, New Visions '94: Honorable Mention, co-sponsored by Voyager Press, Wired Magazine, Interval Corporation **Animation / graphics** Paul Tompkins
Interaction design Marjorie Franklin **Production** Christine Tamblyn **Software used** MMD **Platform** mac

After the opening screen, before the main menu appears, a complete 'how to use' screen appears, clarifying how to navigate and interact with the 'visual self of Tamblyn.

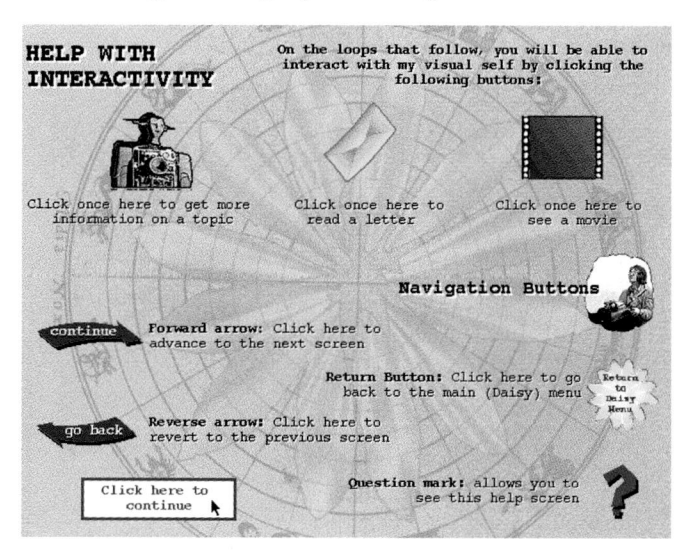

She Loves It, She Loves It Not contains a strong graphic interface using (mostly) twentieth–century images of **robots.** The pictures are presented in collages and work as mood boards. Messages employ a wide variety of 'in your face' screen typography. All the elements interactive technology is claimed to contain – sound, image, text, movement and involvement – are not only present, but also given a fresh interpretation. This work has it own feel and view. It is not technology with a gleam; it has character; it lives.

The first step into Christine's mind brings you to the help screen, a pleasant manual on how to handle this adventure. The fifties **robot icon** indicates that it will elaborate on a topic when clicked, while the graphic of an envelope will reveal a personal reminiscence, hand–written by Christine.

Few female personas operate in cyberspace because of its implications of the dissolution of the body through the computer interface.

A moodboard where all three clickable objects are present. Choosing the robot makes a text statement pop up; clicking the envelope brings up a hand–written letter, and activating the still makes the screen into a small cinema.

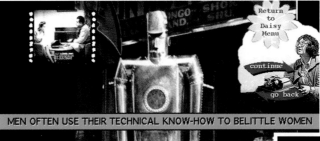

The leaves of a daisy as the interface of the main menu are a friendly and direct metaphor. The petals are the 'buttons', activating a wheel of fortune by displaying a word, like violence, the other and power. The sound of heavy breathing urges the user to continue. Underneath the petals are the mood boards, three to seven per subject. Except for the several clickable icons explained on the help page, nothing is hidden behind the images of this interactive adventure. While the powerful pictures of fifties **pulp science fiction** book covers and commercials evoke an interest in more clickable information, those are not the rules Christine dictated on her help page: what you see is what you get. And what you get are delightful on–screen paintings which tell Christine's story in an utterly thorough and intimate way. She Loves It, She Loves It Not: Women and Technology is a great artistic effort to humanise and personalise the medium of interactivity.

ADAM EEUWENS

69

A story is ended with one strong image to complete the message.

Idea	Building
subjective	objective
abstract	concrete
general	specific
ideal	real
	material

Registros de Arquitectura 1: Mateo at ETH
Vicente Guallart

A classic way of communicating scientific or artistic information is the lecture–with–slides. The professor speaks and explains the background of his illustrations, highlighting interesting details, and maybe answers a question or two, while the students take notes. This format is the starting point for the CD–ROM about the work of Spanish architect Josep Lluis Mateo. We hear him lecture and see the slides. Of course, the CD–ROM offers a lot of extra possibilities: inserting words and captions into the illustrations, graphically highlighting architectural details with colours, **pointers** and lines. There is a (well–)hidden interface that allows one to pause, jump to the next item, review the previous item, or go back to the starting point. A smart feature of this interface is the T button that opens a window to type down notes and comments connected to the work on view — the student's scrapbook.

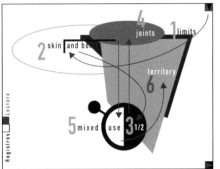

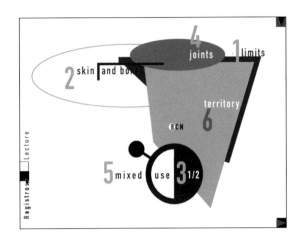

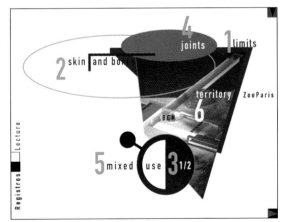

Three versions of the home page (Map) accessing the Lecture and Register sections. When moving the cursor over the numbered areas, photo fragments appear and short quotes are heard.

Title page for the Skin & Bones chapter in the Lecture section. The toolbox above facilitates movement, note–taking and return to the map. As the voice of the architect continues its story, a sequence of slides is shown.

Year of publication 1995 **Author** Vicente Guallart **Place of publication** Barcelona, Spain **Publisher** Producciones New Media SL **Copyright owners** Producciones New Media SL **Awards** Prix Möbius Barcelona '95

Design company Producciones New Media SL **Screen design** Quim Nolla, Daniel Nolla **Animation / graphics** Juan Carlos Ines, Lluis Cantallops, Miquel Beneit **Interaction design** Sergio Schvarstein, Vicente Guallart **Sound design** Nuria Pérez **Production** Gas Newmedia **Editors** Nuria Díaz, Olga Subirós, Thomas Weckerle, Pilar Sinesio **Contributors** Aaron Betsky, Jos Bosman, Kurt Forster, Manel Gausa, Miquel Rodríguez, Joan Iñiguez, Olmo Dalcó, Margarila Burillo **Platform** mac / mpc

mixed use

housing offices

parking

hotel housing

Title page from a chapter in the Register section.

The register is a parallel structure. It gives entry to the 'hard facts' of the buildings that Mateo talks about in his lecture: data, texts, plans, pictures. Where appropriate — in the design for a large-scale building scheme — the interface allows one to **zoom in** on the plan and move it as one moves a large sheet of paper beneath a fixed magnifying glass.

The front page graphically suggests an intimately linked hierarchy of six thematic chapters and offers interactive access to the lecture or to the register that mirrors it. Moving the mouse over this page without clicking activates short **soundbites** and small images to introduce the theme behind each keyword.

Clicking the T option opens a page to write down and store notes.

During the architect's lecture, details in the slides are graphically highlighted.

A slide from the lecture, with the Map option active.

heavy stone

floating

Nowadays, the **limit** is a site of transition, a moment of contact between unrelated realities.

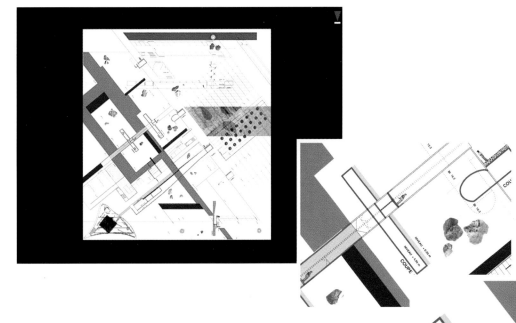

A plan of a large–scale development in the Register section can be magnified. Holding the cursor facilitates moving the map as one moves a sheet of paper under a magnifying glass.

The design stays neatly within the **lecture-slide** metaphor, modestly ordering the screen. Typographical additions only pop up between chapters and when suggested by Mateo's words, thus effectively translating the 'body language' of the pointing and gesturing lecturer into (typo)graphical signs. There is a hint of modernist functionality and transparency in the use of typographical means on this CD–ROM that is very well suited to the architectural language of Mateo's work.

MAX BRUINSMA

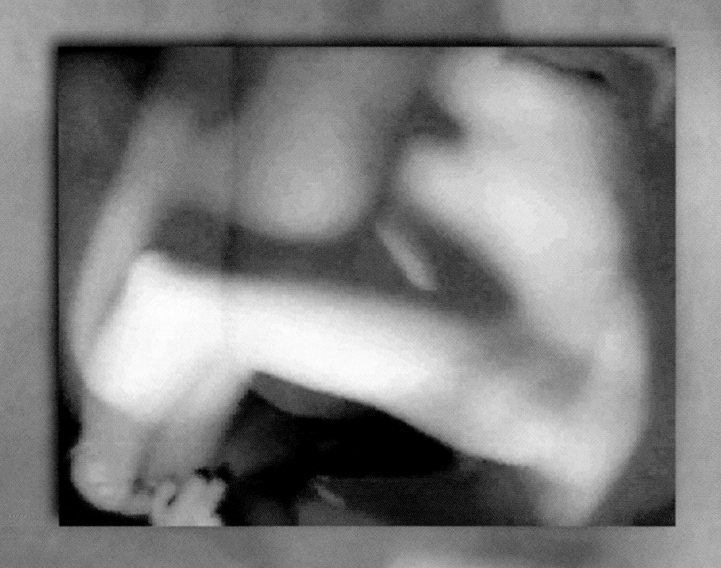

Women at Risk for HIV / Carolyn Sherins

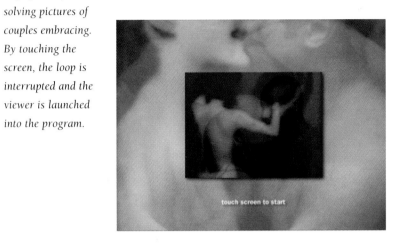

The program's main menu features an icon–based interface that provides access to its various sections. These seven icons are animated in a clockwise direction, indicating them as 'active' buttons.

Women at Risk for HIV is an interactive educational piece designed to raise public awareness about the **danger** of HIV infection among women. Women at Risk is a master's degree project by a student of computer graphics and was designed as a touch–screen public kiosk for such places as shopping malls, record and clothing stores, college campuses and women's health clinics. Geared toward women between the ages of eighteen and thirty, the project takes an unconventional approach to AIDS education, using interactive multimedia to mediate private experiences of infected women and to present women's general attitudes towards HIV infection.

By touching any one of the video–still icons, users can launch a video–taped interview with an HIV positive woman. Highlighted quotes and repeated images add a graphic resonance to selected portions of the interviews.

Year of publication 1995 **Author** Carolyn Sherins **Place of publication** Pasadena, USA **Publisher** Art Center College of Design, Pasadena

Copyright owner Carolyn Sherins **Screen design** Carolyn Sherins **Animation / graphics** Carolyn Sherins

Interaction design Carolyn Sherins **Sound design** Carolyn Sherins **Production** Carolyn Sherins **Editor** Carolyn Sherins **Platform** mac

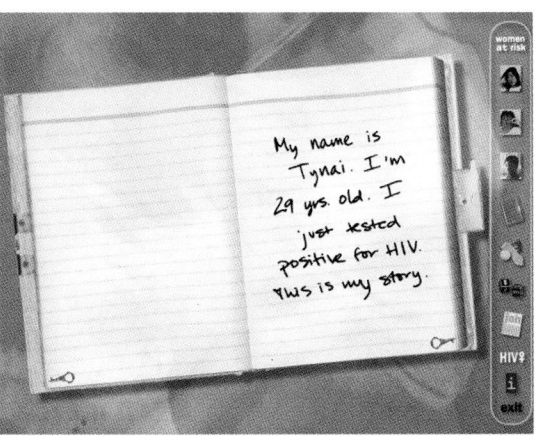

To read through an HIV positive woman's diary, users touch the key to open the book and turn through the pages by touching the keys in their corners. Touching the lock closes the diary.

Women at Risk's opening sequence is both immediate and elusive. When the program is not in use, its screen displays a continual loop of slowly dissolving pictures of couples embracing. These **evocative images** attract passers–by — there are no worded indications of the program's contents. By touching the screen (the words 'touch screen to start' are printed obtrusively towards the screen's bottom) the loop is interrupted and users are launched directly into the program.

An icon–based interface organises the interviews, diaries and conversations that make up the content. In conjunction with the piece's overall graphic treatment, the interface communicates with a certain **directness,** but manages to avoid overpowering the material it presents. The first screen introduces the title and a range of animated icons through which users can access the various areas. These icons are arranged along the side of every screen that follows to allow easy movement within the program.

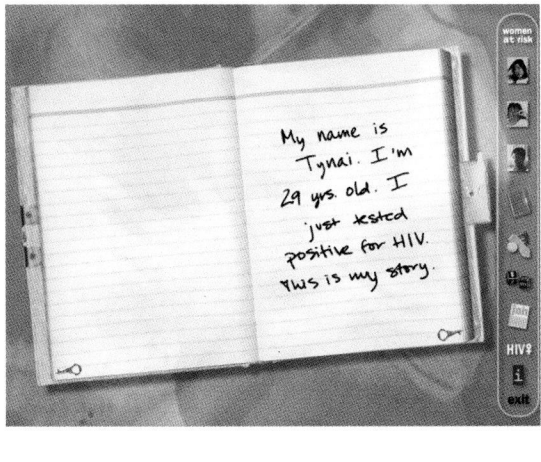

Condom Talk is a refreshingly light–hearted sequence in which colourful condoms dance across the screen. Any of the condoms may be touched — this prompts them to unroll from their packages — to hear excerpts from women's conversations on the subject.

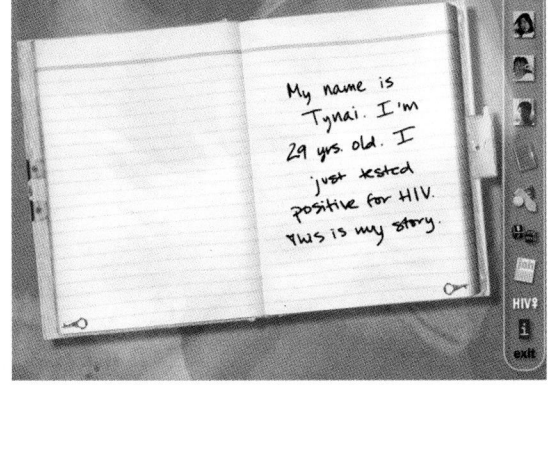

Sequences include video–taped interviews with HIV–positive women, an HIV–infected woman's **diary** that can be paged through, a section that focuses on women's attitudes towards using condoms, a questionnaire to determine women's attitudes towards safe sex and a section on HIV testing. Graphic styles are influenced by the tone of the dialogue in each sequence. For example, in the sequence on condoms, colourful condoms dance across the screen and unroll when touched, while gossipy exchanges about women's experiences with them are overheard. The visual style here is refreshingly light–hearted, compared with other areas whose emotionally overpowering narratives require more conventional graphic treatments.

While Women at Risk conveys a sense of graphically heightened drama — particularly in its typographic treatments — the program avoids preaching and alarmist tactics. The designer's choice of essentially **low-tech** aesthetics makes the project all the more distinguished.

Melissa Dallal

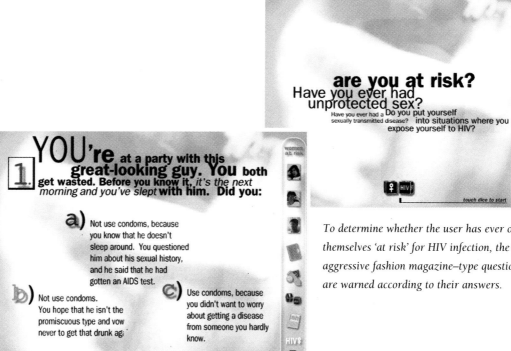

To determine whether the user has ever or would be likely to put themselves 'at risk' for HIV infection, the program employs an aggressive fashion magazine–type questionnaire in which users are warned according to their answers.

77

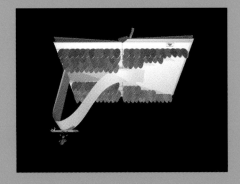

Pop Up Computer, ASK/TX/SOFTX/SARU Brunei, 1994

Family

Easy is the magic word when it comes to family life — virtual family life, that is, the life of pleasure and play, of fantasy and 'infotainment'. Teaching toddlers how to operate their first mouse, chasing cats and dogs along the screen; chatting with your neighbours on another continent; fighting monsters that politely say game over when they've devoured you...

The screen says: easy. It leads you into a world of fantasy that eventually may become uneasy, as part of a game, but always grants you a second chance. There is a goal somewhere — there is always a goal somewhere — but the interaction is devoted to your entertainment as long as you are underway. And to get there again by another way.

The CD–ROM greatly enhances the possibility of combining play and learning for children. The do–it–on–screen brick boxes and colouring books talk back to the kids and guide them through a playroom full of games and stories that sing them songs, praise them when they are good and gently console them when something goes wrong. More than video and TV, which invite passive consumption or dull zapping, CD–ROMs demand active participation from the child. The medium can be a great help for parents and nannies; it keeps the kid occupied and the place clean.

Multimedia for family purposes mirror the existing media: television, video, comic books, magazines and games. Graphic design for family titles also draws from the repertoire of the existing media: a cool flow of information that should not look too much like work.

Bright colours and optimistic imagery, laid out with a smile. Each stage of the process should be designed to please and entice. The screen is replete with signs that arouse curiosity and hidden surprises. Every appealing detail triggers a click reflex that is rewarded with a sound or a song, a short animation or another turn of the tale. The screen is a different place, not a community room where you share the experience of watching TV, listening to records or playing games around a table. The screen keeps you busy in a room of your own — not lonely, but away from the madding crowd... The main task of design here is to keep things going smoothly. As long as it is easy to continue on one's way, it does not have to be easy to reach one's goal.

MAX BRUINSMA

79

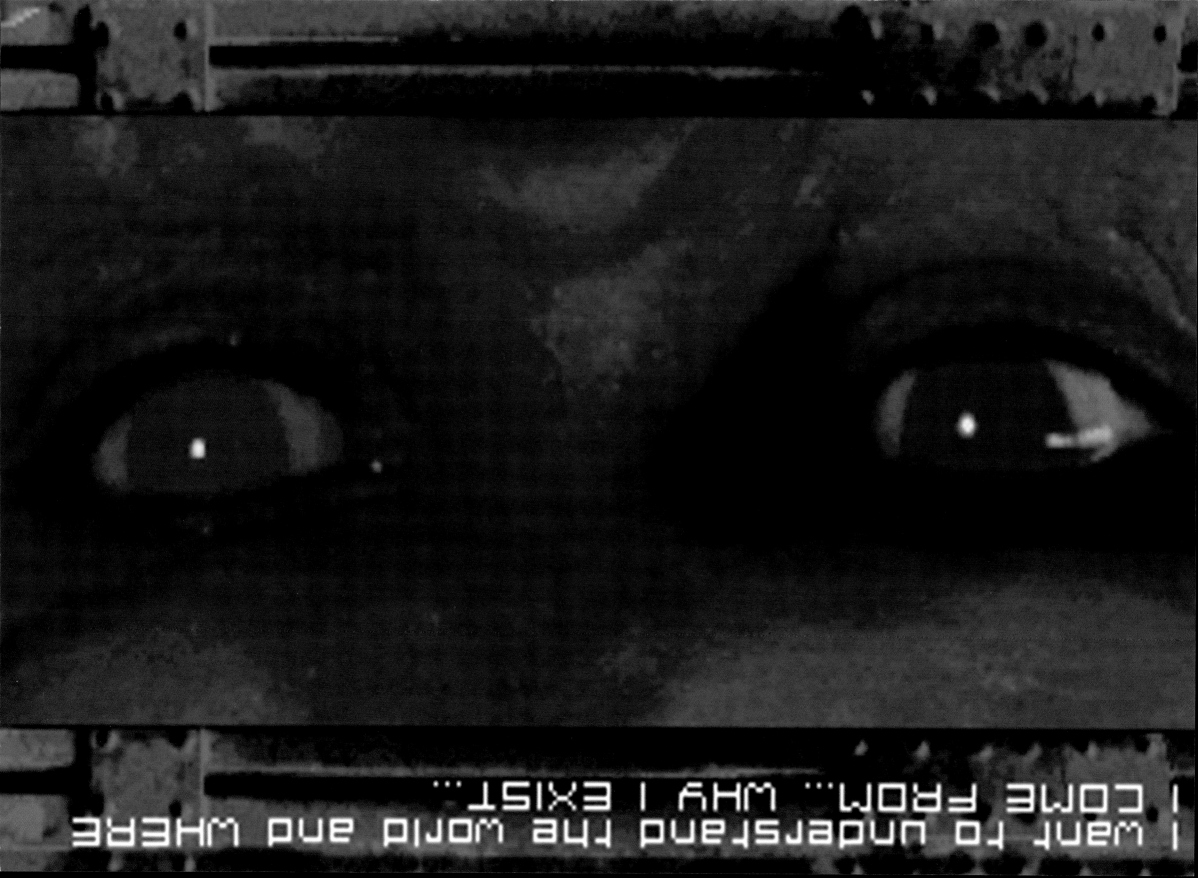

I want to understand the world and WHERE I COME FROM... WHY I EXIST...

Captain Blood is being preserved in a semi–cryogenic state. He can only see through part of his helmet. Therefore (and probably for the convenience of the designer) the player can only see him in the same way.

Commander Blood / Cryo Interactive Entertainment

All spaceship functions are accessed by touching coloured balls (pressing buttons). In this case, a message has come in on the ship's videophone. You can answer by pressing the orange button.

Amazing new technologies: hit the orange ball with the virtual hand (lower right). The ball rolls into space and the player is warped to a new destination.

Every trip to a planet's surface comes in different psychedelic colours. Some of them look more like near–death experiences than standard, space–to–surface movements.

Space and extraterrestrial cultures pose an obvious problem for the designer: as no–one knows how life in **space** really looks, it is impossible for designers to portray it accurately. Of course, designers can extrapolate what mankind already seems to know about space, but this generally produces a rather dull picture: as far as we know at present, space is big, cold and devoid of life as we are able to recognise it.

Science fiction writers have always solved these problems as only writers are allowed to: by not considering the reality of space at all. Writers simply described space as they imagined it. The individual reader's imagination was all that was needed to accept the strange new worlds and alien technologies invented by the writer.

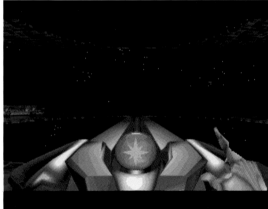

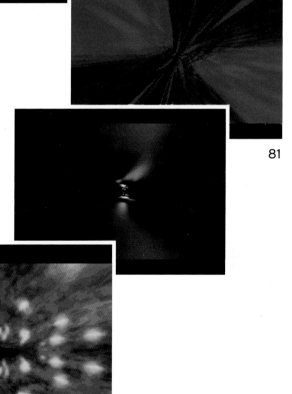

Year of publication 1994 **Author** Cryo Interactive Entertainment **Place of publication** France, USA **Publisher** Microfolie's Éditions **Copyright owners** Microfolie's, Cryo **Awards** Prix Canal+ Imagina '95

Design company Cryo Interactive Entertainment **Screen design** Marcello Mora, Didier Bouchon **Animation / graphics** Franck Dorel, Philippe Arbogast, Sébastien Guilbers, Jean-Jacques Chaubin

Interaction design Olivier Carado, Didier Bouchon, Philippe Ulrich **Sound design** Stéphane Picq, Philippe Égret **Production** Cryo Interactive Entertainment **Editors** Microfolie's Éditions **Contributors** Philippe Ulrich **Platform** mpc

Ready for a touchdown on Moskito, a bug planet of course.

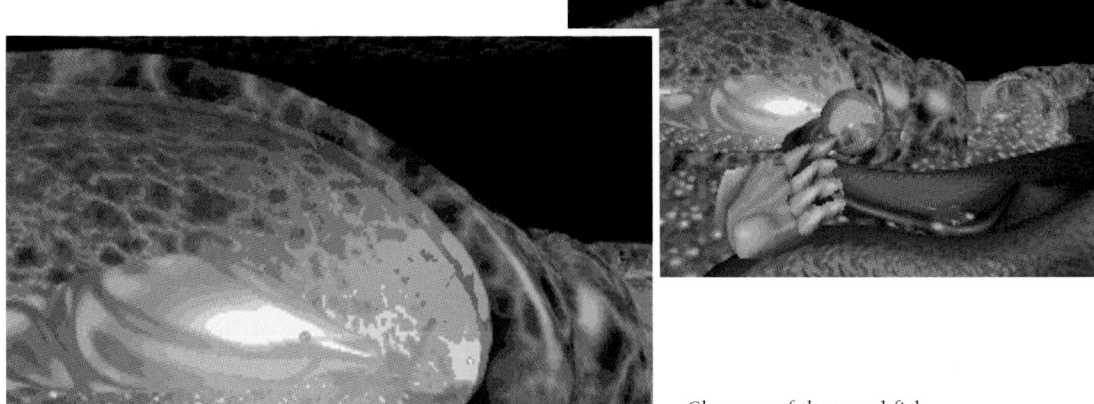

The travel fish is standing by on the left.

Close–up of the travel fish.

Commander Blood is one of the most bizarre space fantasies to be invented in this way. In this space adventure game, the player travels through space in a kind of living spaceship. Leader of the crew is Captain Bob, a 70.000–year–old creature who is trying to solve the mysteries of time, space and the **big bang** by exploring black holes. During the game, Commander Blood travels to all kinds of strange new worlds inhabited by even stranger creatures. These creatures invariably want the Commander to perform one or more tasks for them, such as buying meat on a butcher planet or repairing an overloaded guard robot on a junkyard planet. In exchange, Blood receives money, nice high–tech goodies and — most importantly — co–ordinates of new planets to visit.

Although the world of Commander Blood is completely imaginary, certain conventions inevitably recur. For example, all creatures have arms, legs, eyes and a mouth; all of the planets are basically round; everyone is looking for a **better life** and nothing is free. It seems that even the wildest fantasies cannot exist without a tight reference to life as we know it.

The visor of an overloaded robo–guard.

This space rat wants you to buy meat. If you want to know more about his species, just point to a subject you're interested in.

The butcher on the meat planet is a busy creature. The rats who ordered the meat will have to wait a little longer.

Blood's means of transportation to his various destinations is a wonderful combination of **psychedelic** space fantasy and virtual reality technologies. The player sees a hand on a screen, much like the hand people would see in the eighties when they put on a dataglove and virtual reality–helmet. Hitting one of several balls causes the spaceship to travel to a certain part of space. The player then must touch one of the planets with the hand. He descends to the surface of the planet through the mouth of a space fish.

Once on the planet, things really get weird. Rats ask the player to buy them meat; monsters party thirty-six hours a day; **virus-infected** robots try to shoot the player. In short, everything a player with a feel for psychedelics can dream up will happen, too! Is there a catch? Perhaps this is an accurate portrayal of life in space. Who knows?

BEN DE DOOD

The spaceship comes with fourteen different TV channels.

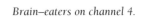

Brain–eaters on channel 4.

Pink monsters rule the ether on channel one.

Pink monsters? Everybody knows a good monster is green.

The strangest creatures of them all: humans.

83

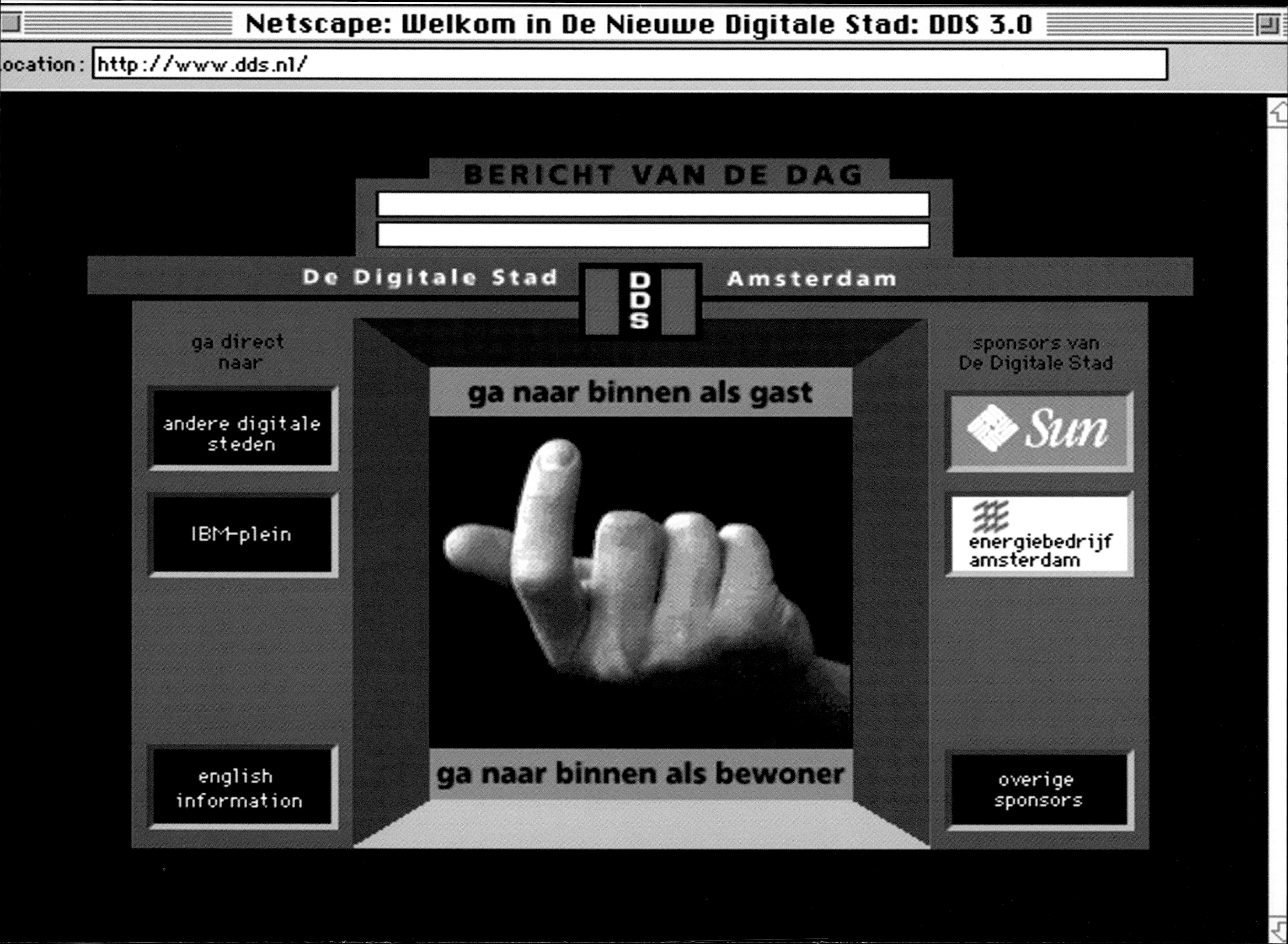

Netscape: Welkom in De Nieuwe Digitale Stad: DDS 3.0

Location: http://www.dds.nl/

BERICHT VAN DE DAG

De Digitale Stad **DDS** Amsterdam

ga direct naar

andere digitale steden

IBM-plein

english information

ga naar binnen als gast

ga naar binnen als bewoner

sponsors van De Digitale Stad

Sun

energiebedrijf amsterdam

overige sponsors

The Digital City 3.0 / Stichting De Digitale Stad

DDS Central, the service centre of the digital town, where the octagon contains all the technical data required.

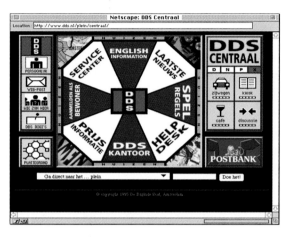

An example of a square, in this case the film. The car on the side links to sidepaths, or other related sites. The glass takes you to a cafe.

This is the map of the town. The octagons are the squares of the town, holding topic–related sites. The small squares in the middle contain the houses of individuals.

DDS 3.0, The Digital City 3.0, the on–line equivalent of the City of Amsterdam, is a site on the World Wide Web. More than five thousand people access this spot every day. More than thirty thousand people have their mailboxes here and more than a million hits are registered per month. So the makers of this site had the consider-able task of making it an attractive **place to live** in; for the inhabitants, the companies and the services of the City Council. And for all the newcomers and visitors.

One square holds the park.

A sample page of the place where the indi-viduals have their house or homepage; people can live near the square of their interest.

Year of publication 1995 **Author** Stichting De Digitale Stad **Place of publication** http://www.dds.nl **Publisher** Stichting De Digitale Stad **Copyright owners** The Digital City

Design company The Digital City (De Digitale Stad) **Screen design** Marjolein Ruyg **Animation / graphics** Marjolein Ruyg **Interaction design** Rob van der Haar

Production Marleen Stikker, Joost Flint **Editors** Marleen Stikker, Joost Flint **Soft- and hardware** Michael van Eeden, Erwin Bolwidt **Platform** www

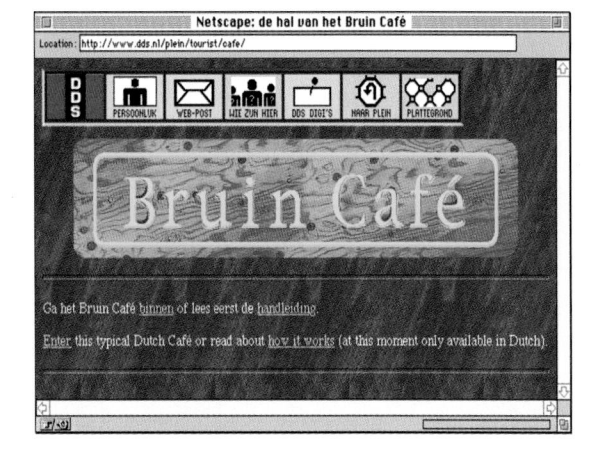

Every square has its own cafe where people can meet to chat.

The first thing you want when visiting a strange city is to find your way around and to feel secure while doing so. When arriving at the gateway to The Digital City 3.0, an inviting hand beckons you to come in. An **octagon** appears, the main square of the town, holding eight slices of information fields covering easy-to-use service and informational sites. One can join or choose to browse on as guest.

In the main picture corners, pictograms offer passage to other squares of the on–line city.

Examples of the variety of people held by the homepages in The Digital City 3.0.

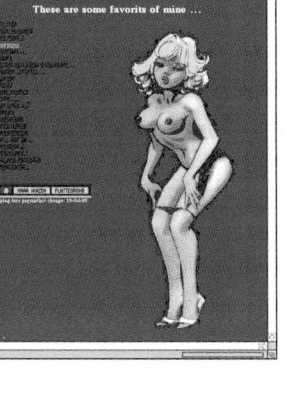

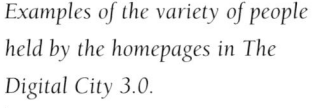

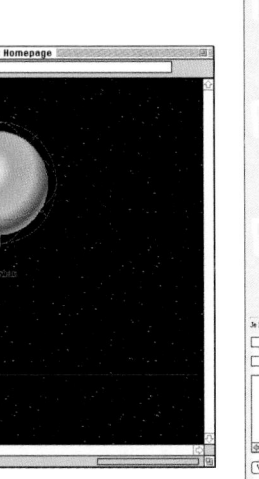

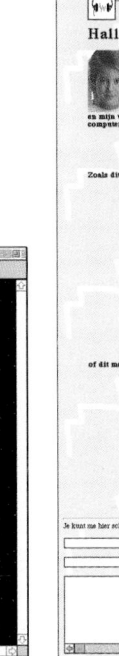

There are only squares in this town. Houses form the connecting elements. On the map, the squares and their connectors resemble the diagram of a molecule. A small picture defines their field of interest. The square enlarges when clicked upon and the octagon re-appears, divided into eight slices, each containing a subject–related site. On the sides of the octagon are fields which hold the homepages of individual inhabitants.

Icons which are always present at the side of the main window allow users to interact with the people on the square they are visiting. The pictogram of a car offers a sidepath or links to other sites on a topic, the **wineglass** icon transports you to the cafe, where the people in this part of town meet and chat. On the left, one finds the map, the envelope to send mail, places a personal ad or inquires who else is present.

The Digital City 3.0, already a perfect metaphor for an on–line community, has an organic, natural feel to it. Anyone can intuitively find their way through the layers of information, from general to specific. Everyone feels **at home** here– one can find the 'homepages' of children and complete families in DDS 3.0 – within an hour. This is an important and major accomplishment.

ADAM EEUWENS

Dragon Lore / Cryo Interactive Entertainment

The cow is stuck so tightly to the player that it seems as if the computer has crashed in some strange way.

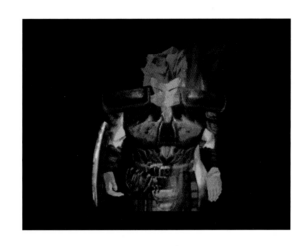

Some things never change, like the punishment for a mistake: death by burning. The game is over.

89

Dragon Lore shows how far graphics in computer games have evolved since the early days of Pong and Donkey Kong. It starts off very impressively with a gorgeously rendered **movie** about an evil knight who harasses an innocent king and his new–born son. The son is secretly brought to a safe place, a farm-house owned by a simple but friendly peasant. There, the young prince awaits the day of his vengeance.

Isn't this strange? All the participants get to have their close–up at least once.

The great surprise starts immediately after the game begins: the graphics are of the same beautiful quality as the introduction movie itself. There is virtually no loss of quality after the player enters the **mythical** country.

A devil's servant greets the player. The morning star greets back from a first person viewpoint.

Year of publication 1995 Author Cryo Interactive Entertainment Place of publication France Publisher Mindscape Copyright owners Mindscape International, Cryo Interactive Entertainment

Design company Cryo Interactive Entertainment Screen design Jean Luc Sala, Olivier Ledroit Animation / graphics Rachid Mékaoui, Sandrine Houalet, Philippe Nouhra, David Hégo, Claudine Roussard, Yvon Trévien

Interaction design Fabrice Bernard, Yvon Trévien, David Hégo Sound design Stéphane Picq Production Cryo Interactive Entertainment Editors Mindscape Game design François Marcella Froideval, Jahan Robson Platform dos

The hero of the game is accompanied by a small, cute dragon that replaces the usual, dull mouse pointer. Initially, most players are confused by the little animal, because it is so well done that it is not immediately recognisable as a mouse pointer. Apart from a few **little jokes**, the game is actually quite serious. There are skeletons to be killed (in 3D, from the player's viewpoint), riddles to be solved and treasures to be discovered.

The player's interaction with his character on screen is surprisingly simple and efficient. Dragon Lore is a full–screen game. There is not even so much as a row of icons taking up valuable screen space. To access the hero's possessions, the player simply clicks on the right–mouse button when the mouse pointer (or should one say dragon pointer?) is at the top of the screen. The game pauses and the hero is displayed from top to bottom with his **possessions** at his side. To let the hero use one of the items, players simply drag it to his hand. To get a description of the item, it is held in front of his eyes and clicked once again. This is all the interface the player gets. It is also all the interface the player really needs.

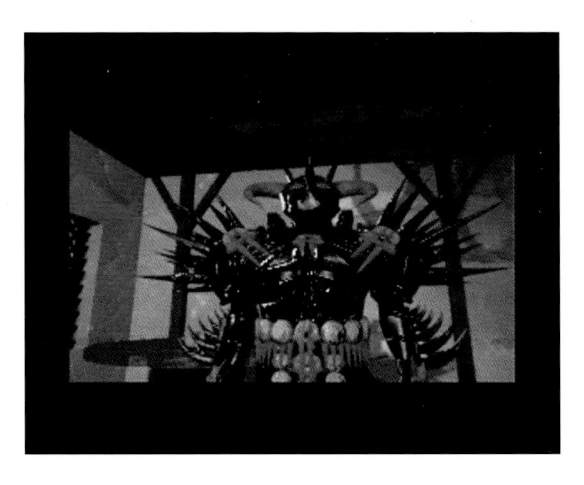

The evil knight in all his glory. The nice part is: he doesn't even pixelize when in close–up.

The majestic dragon lands on the castle. The player is amazed at its beauty.

90

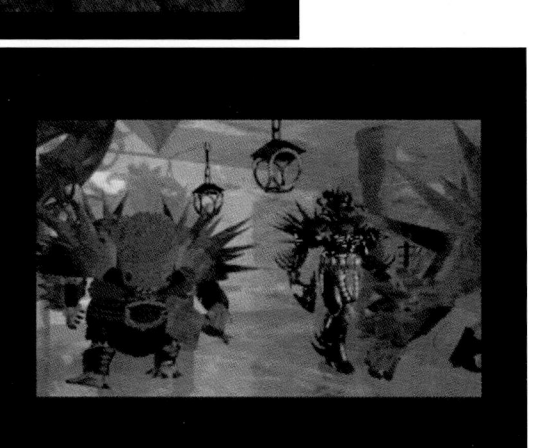

The servants actually are more impressive than their master.

What are these devils so taken with bull's horns, anyway?

Every now and then, the graphics are replaced by a short movie. For example, when the hero has to make a long journey, instead of having to click to his destination, the player only has to do the first few steps. Then the program takes over and shows a short movie of the trip. A few steps before the player's arrival, the movie stops and the program goes back into player mode, without any change in graphic quality. This player found it downright **miraculous**: just one, tiny step away from the virtual reality version of the game.

BEN DE DOOD

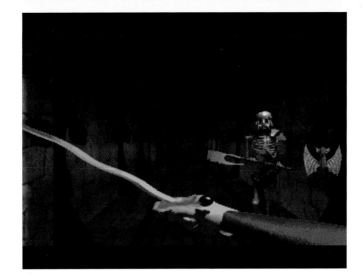

The player strikes out to kill the dead.

Don't worry, they're just road signs, really.

Mushroom City (what else?)

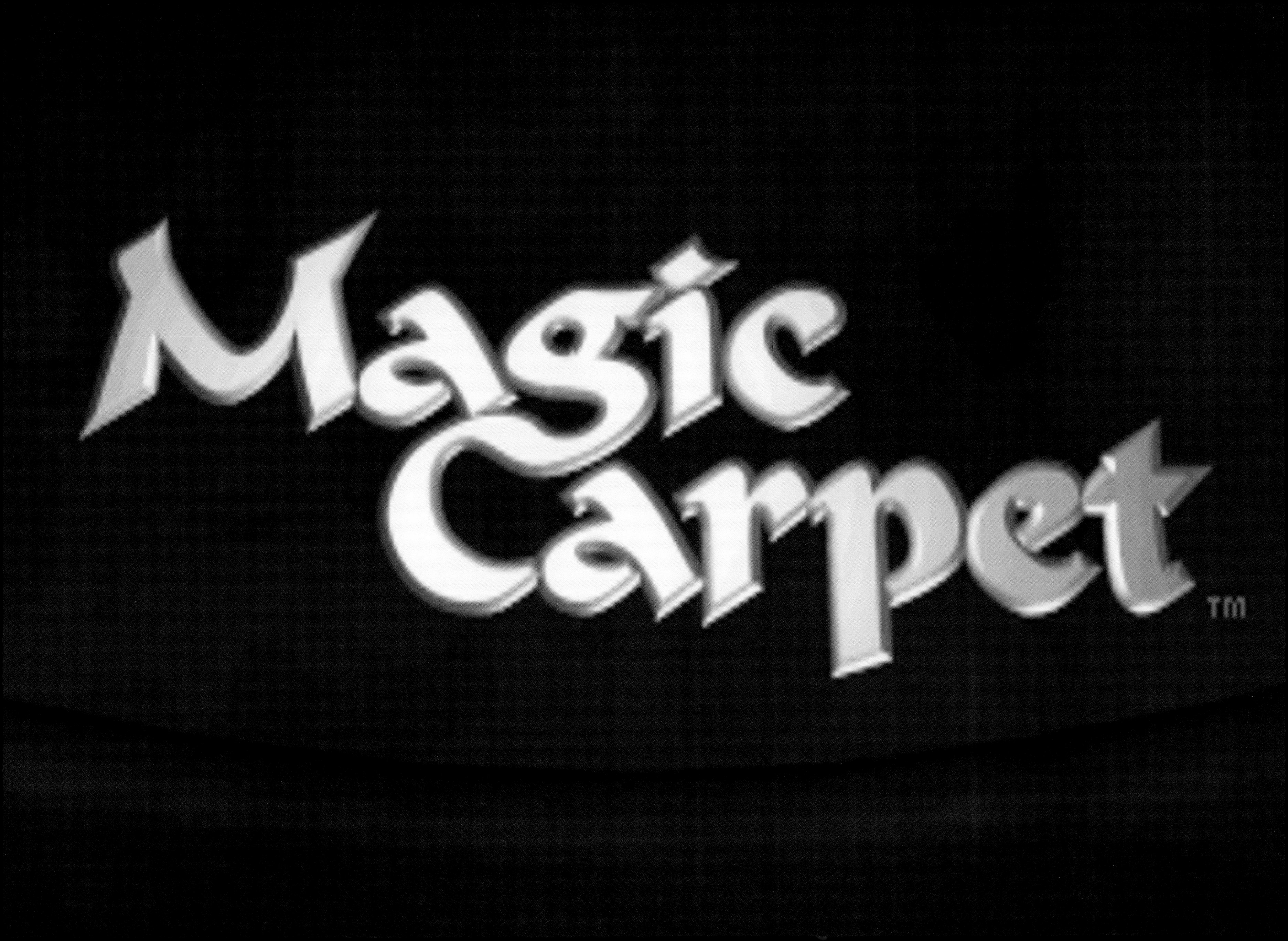
Magic Carpet™

Magic Carpet / Bullfrog Productions

Through the years, gamers have been introduced to a wide variety of different interfaces, all of which were intended to make the game easy to play and obviate the necessity of studying an extensive manual. Games designers tried virtually everything in their **quest** for the ultimate gaming interface: pull–up and pull–down menus, menus that popped out of the sides of the screen, inventory boxes that cluttered the screen, leaving little room for the game itself, middle and right mouse buttons with a variety of gaming functions, hot spots, mouse pointers in every possible shape and huge amounts of icons that nobody really seemed to understand. Sometime in 1994, the amount of gaming help functions reached its peak and was followed by a turnabout. Designers went back to basics and started experimenting with 'intuitive' and **'minimal'** design. This soon resulted in the complete disappearance of the visible gaming interface. At the very most, a single help screen remained for the convenience of the gamer. For the rest, it was up to the gamers themselves, and they didn't need to be told twice. After all, gaming rule number one still is: figure it out by yourself.

The story of Magic Carpet is supposed to be an ancient Arabian tale, once recorded in a book containing 1001 different stories. In keeping with this idea, the game begins with drawings instead of a movie.

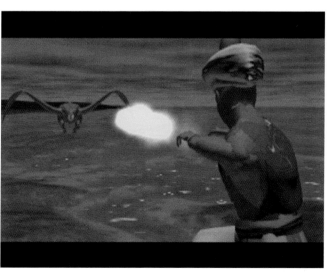

Since Magic Carpet is not really a book, but a game played on a computer, the drawings can come alive. The magic starts.

93

An enemy dragon attacks the palace.

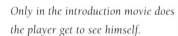

How does it fly without a magic carpet, one wonders.

Only in the introduction movie does the player get to see himself.

Year of publication 1994 **Author** Bullfrog Productions **Place of publication** UK **Publisher** Bullfrog Productions **Copyright owners** Microfolie's, Cryo

Awards Ects Awards: Game of the Year '94 Germany and France, Computer Software Game of the Year '94, Most Original New Title '94, Spotlight Award Games Developer Conference '94

Design company Bullfrog Productions **Animation / graphics** Paul McLaughlin, Michael Man, Mark Healey, Chriss Hill, Finolay McGechie, Eoin Rogan, Barry Meade, Tony Dawson **Interaction design** Glen Corpes

Sound design Russell Shaw **Production** Peter Molyneux, Sean Cooper **Editors** Mark Huntley, Simon Carter, Phil Jones **Contributors** Sean Masterson, Barry Meade, Alex Trovers, Jonty Barnes, Daniel Russel **Platform** dos

This new austerity meant that designers had to be even more cautious, because every extra function might entail an extra amount of 'screen pollution'. At the same time, the lack of a visible interface left **more room** for the game images themselves. In fact, the use of the complete screen required designers to work much as if for a television screen instead of a computer monitor.

Enter Magic Carpet. In this shoot-em-up game, the player assumes the role of an 'Arabian Nights' magician's apprentice. He is charged with restoring the world to equilibrium. To reach this goal, the apprentice has to kill all kinds of walking, swimming and flying creatures and steal back their **energy.** A creature can be killed by shooting it with a variety of ammunition like stones, lightning, fire, etcetera. When a creature dies, its energy is freed in the form of red balls. By changing the colour of these balls (shooting them with magic paint in the form of white crystals), the player acquires their energy, ready to use for good instead of evil.

The only help screen the player gets, with a map on the left, a small view of the big screen (top right), and icons of all the weapons the magician can find. Nothing more is needed.

Keep an eye on the volcanoes. Their eruptions change the landscape completely, in real time.

The player cannot see himself on his carpet, but in 'more player mode', the other magicians become visible. Except for their colours, they all look the same.

Three huge earthworms preparing to attack.

The young magician travels on a flying carpet. The player controls the carpet and various weapons with a game pad, a joy–stick or a combination of mouse and keyboard.

Of course, Magic Carpet is not the only successful full–screen game that is easily playable without a visible interface. It is not even the first or only PC game also playable in **virtual reality,** but it is one of a select group of 3D games that show images of monsters in such a way that they actually scare the gamer, even when the immersion in the gaming world goes no further than being seated in front of a flat, 14–inch screen. For an outsider it may seem to be 'only a game', but for gamers, it is sheer magic.

BEN DE DOOD

Don't hurt these villagers. It is against the rules of the game. Besides, they may avenge themselves by destroying your castle.

Balloons are used to transport the regained energy to the safety of the castle.

95

The enemy has evoked an army of the dead. Fortunately, they cannot alter the colour of the white, regained energy balls.

Calling all enemies. For the player's safety, land and sky are usually simultaneously visible.

P.A.W.S : Personal Automated Wagging System
Domestic Funk Products

Centred on your canine POV, relatively non–abstract icons control all other action, from Sleep (night sky) to the basic doggy actions (Sniff, Dig, Eat and three degrees of Bark) and access to Bone map and Dog Anatomy section.

The big, bright icons in the opening menu are about as complicated as the P.A.W.S. interface gets. A low level of required mouse skill throughout reflects its young target group without sacrificing the charm of interaction.

P.A.W.S. — the Personal Automated Wagging System — is a simple idea, realised so completely, with such charm, skill, wit and imagination as to immediately place it in a league of its own. It is a compellingly **daft,** goal–free adventure game that appeals to adults and young alike.

Comprising three basic sections: Dog Anatomy, an **Aerodogs** game and Navigation, it is the latter in which most of the action takes place. Essentially a 'dog simulator', P.A.W.S. takes the user inside the mind of man's best friend — complete with low attention span and limited motivation (basically chasing, eating and leg–cocking).

The action–reaction relationship is as sharp as the colours. Here, the clickable map gives a dog's–eye view of bones hidden in a yard. Find and eat them to keep the bone meter (bottom right) in the red.

One of the amusing dream sequences of P.A.W.S.; below, left, right and centre, are the movement and action icons.

97

Year of publication 1994 **Author** Domestic Funk Products **Place of publication** New York, USA **Publisher** Organa **Copyright owners** Domestic Funk Products, Hup! Multimedia

Awards Milia d'Or '95: British Interactive Multimedia Association Gold Award for Best Children's Title 1995, Macformat Classic **Design company** Domestic Funk Products

Screen design Domestic Funk Products, Nick Batt, Alan Snow, David Furlow **Animation / graphics** Alan Snow **Interaction design** Domestic Funk Products **Sound design** Nick Batt

Production Domestic Funk Products **Editors** Domestic Funk Products, Nick Batt, Alan Snow, David Furlow **Contributors** Domestic Funk Products, Nick Batt, Alan Snow, David Furlow **Software used** MMD **Platform** mac / mpc

Thirty-five thousand frames of beautiful animation ensure a huge range of outcomes to each journey. Animator/graphic designer Alan Snow's How Dogs Work (the New York Times Best Children's Book of 1993) is the blueprint. The graphic style is reminiscent of the **anarchic** seventies TV cartoon Roobarb and Custard, and there is a fun pastiche of the Thunderbirds countdown sequence to start the Aerodogs game. Unlike so many CD-ROMs, it looks like it was a lot of fun to make.

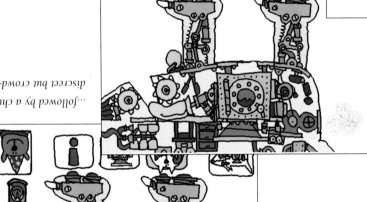

The representation of the messy 'wetware' of a living dog in a mechanistic, engineered style offers plenty of opportunities for humour throughout the disk. Though science fiction offers the prospect of robo-pets, an imaginary robo-dog is already realisable with imagination, a childhood attribute often undervalued in CD titles.

Each trip as a virtual dog begins upon waking. Outside the kennel lies a multi-coloured 3D garden environment, with next door's **cat to chase**, postmen to bite, bones to sniff out and chomp, ponds and garden borders to plunge into, all via simple movement icons, basic actions (Sniff, Dig, Scoff) and noise buttons (a repertoire of Yip, Snarl and Whimper).

The internal workings of a dog as represented by Domestic Funk Productions. Click on the bowels, legs, filing cabinet memory or anywhere else for a witty and illuminating animated explanation.

No mistaking the part of the canine body being demonstrated here. Clicking Eat triggers an animated gobble and swallow...

...followed by a churning alimentation, and ending with a discreet but crowd-pleasing pool at the end.

Inside the canine brain, a simple world view is reflected. Here, the dog's memory bank, Cat section, P.A.W.S, succeeds, where many children's titles fail, in establishing a distinctive and rich view of its world, characters' personalities and foibles, through graphics alone.

Audio designer and programmer Nick Batt (similarly distinguished in the music business) does a great job. Economical, witty and apposite, the sound goes beyond effects; sound and vision are so well–knitted as to effectively produce one synaesthetic medium: Dogvision. There is no text or even spoken language – you're a dog, right? And like a dog, neglect your **bone finding** and your energy level will fall; sleep — and maybe canine dreams — will overtake you.

P.A.W.S. is earthy in the way kids really love, but never coarse. Too many developers of children's software act as though 'child–like' and 'infantile' are synonymous. Here are no cutesy 'Disneyfication', patronising voice–overs or saccharine–coated pedagogical bores; rather, P.A.W.S. simply aims to draw its target four– to six– year–olds into a **fantasy world** in which they can play with fundamental concepts of spatial relationships, navigation and free–form imagination.

Judging by this first title, Domestic Funk Productions epitomises all that was promised would be good about the nascent multimedia industry: independent, **bursting** with originality and creativity, solidly grounded creatives capable of title concepts unrealisable in old media. I await the Virtual Cat sequel with anticipation.

JULES MARSHALL

A simple game section of P.A.W.S. gives the user six sniffs (the tea-cup shapes in the dog's head) at hidden smells to identify what's under the lid. The consistency of the dog's inner workings add to the overall believability of the interface and its metaphors.

Up, up and away; lift–off for the Aerodog, following a Thunderbirds–style countdown.

99

The dog flies around, using the icons. The scrolling landscape is reversible, so no complaints about left–to–right masculine bias with this game.

And at the end, you get a bone rating from your fellow 'aerodogs'. Probably a nice introduction to cause and effect and spatial relationships for the very young.

POK the Little "Artiste" / Arborescence

Almost every object in this picture hides a game of some sort. Just click and play.

The first rule that must be followed when designing educational games for little children is the old mechanic's dictum **KISS:** Keep It Simple, Stupid! This doesn't mean that the material must always be as simple as adding one and one. It does mean that the learning process itself should be so easy that it is only after the learning experience that the child realises he or she has actually learned something, as if the nice storytellers reveal themselves to be teachers only after the book is closed. In nineties terms, we call this 'user friendliness'.

Hide the animals on the floor in a corresponding painting.

Some things seem easy, like the question: which little fish is the offspring of the big fish? (But just wait until your kid asks why and how!).

Year of publication 1994 **Author** Arborescence **Place of publication** Paris, France **Publisher** Arborescence **Copyright owners** Arborescence **Design company** Arborescence

Screen design Michel Prudhomme, Pascal Valdes **Animation / graphics** Michel Prudhomme, Pascal Valdes **Interaction design** Gilbert Amar, Sébastien Burel, Patrick Soquet

Sound design François Banger **Production** Arborescence **Editors** Michel Prudhomme, Pascal Valdes **Contributors** Michel Prudhomme, Pascal Valdes **Software used** AMT **Platform** mac / mpc

Recognising similar forms in the sky and in the water.

Fill the fish bowls with water. It's deceptively simple.

User friendliness for personal computers in this day and age means: let the user use a mouse to access all the information contained in the CD–ROM; don't use many different icons; don't hide the menus and (since the invention of multimedia) don't write it down if you can say it.

The designers of POK have understood all this very well. They have made every effort not to intimidate the children. POK The Little "Artiste" starts with a cute little interface in the form of a child's drawing of an orange, a leopard, a sun, a fish, a house and some sort of robot. A **little monkey** with a funny voice tells the player what to do (just click on one of the drawings).

Colouring books aren't what they used to be. Even the kid's hands stay clean. (There goes half the fun!)

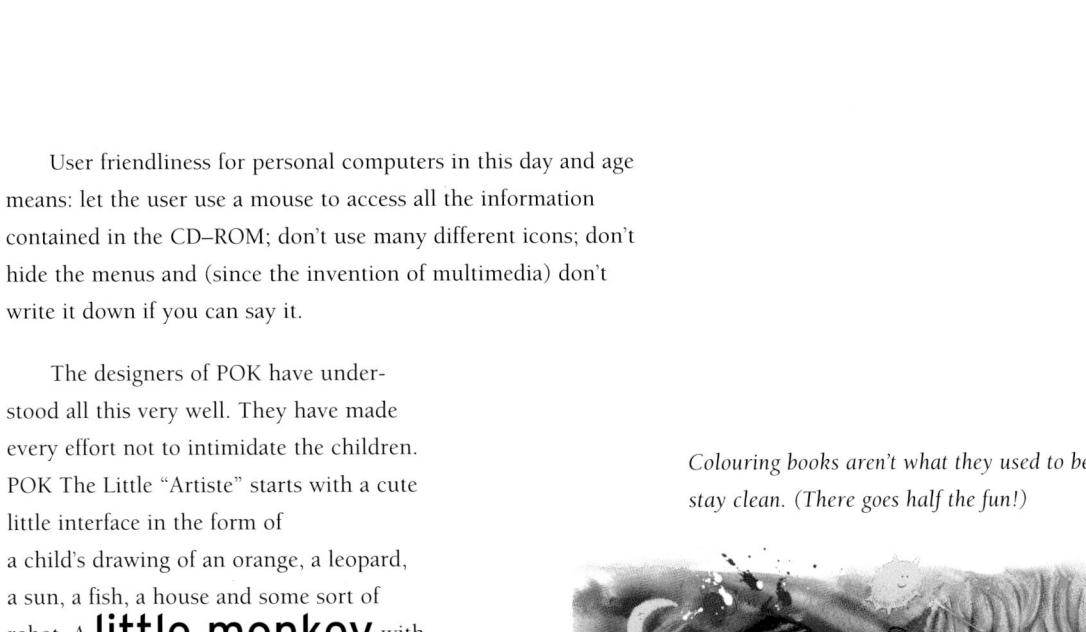

Let's annoy the monkey by changing the landscape it is trying to draw. Just click on one of the weather symbols and watch the monkey tear off the drawing in progress.

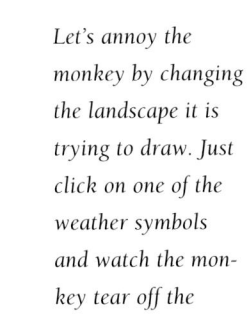

Games follow in which the player has to recognise colours by smashing coloured pumpkins onto heads of ghosts and make fruit juice by playing with a fruit machine. Pattern recognition is learned in a game in which the player has to hide animals inside paintings hanging on a wall. There is a time limit: when the keeper comes back and there are still some animals in sight, the keeper gets mad and the game is lost. Simple traffic rules and more **colour** recognition are learned in a game in which you have to guide a robot down a coloured road to a tent by clicking on corresponding colours. Simple, isn't it?

To top it all off, the 'big' games are accompanied by small but funny games and gadgets. An umbrella starts spinning when clicked on; snow falls out of the sky when the player clicks on a small drawing of a boy in swimming trousers. Even some sort of genetic engineering is learned when the player is asked which **little fish** is most probably the offspring of papa fish and mama fish. Ah, well, one is never too young to learn.

BEN DE DOOD

Click on the cloud above the boy in the swimming trunks.

Fortunately, the designers remembered that not only installation should be easy.

103

Learning the colours or traffic rules? Why not both at the same time?

Pop Up Computer

Gento Matsumoto, Saru Brunei

Pop Up Computer is a computer–simulated **pop up book** on CD–ROM. To view its contents, users must engage the book as a physical object by turning its pages to reveal the individual pop up spreads with colourful and precisely rendered 3D graphics. Not surprisingly, in addition to celebrating what can be done with the printed page, the program also allows users to enter into and interact with the individual pop up spreads. With the help of sound and animation, these spreads take on a life of their own and present exciting realms for exploration.

To begin Pop Up Computer, users must first open the book and continue turning its pages until they reach the Table of Contents. At that point, there is the option to leaf through the book page by page or to select an alphabet letter that will transport users to its corresponding spread.

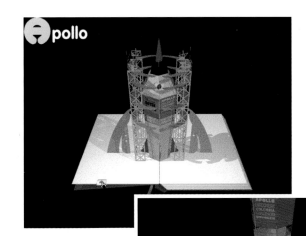

Featured under 'A' for Apollo, this first of the program's twenty–six spreads enacts a space shuttle launch whose success or failure is determined at random by the computer.

Year of publication 1994 **Author** Gento Matsumoto, Saru Brunei **Place of publication** Tokyo, Japan **Publisher** ASK, TX, SOFTX **Copyright owners** ASK, TX, SOFTX, Saru Brunei **Awards** Minister of International Trade and Industry Award '94, Yomiuri Press Award '94, International Digital Media Award '94 **Design company** ASK, TX, SOFTX, Saru Brunei **Screen design** Gento Matsumoto, Saru Brunei **Animation / graphics** Gento Matsumoto, Saru Brunei **Interaction design** Gento Matsumoto, Saru Brunei **Sound design** Gento Matsumoto, Saru Brunei **Production** ASK, Saru Brunei **Editors** ASK, Saru Brunei **Contributors** ASK, Saru Brunei, H. Tokiwa; Tokyo Kousaku Club, E. Ikematsu, T. Suzuki, M. Samata, E. Ikematsu, M. Buffalo Daughter, H. Tachibana, Net Shop Boys, S. Takemura **Platform** mac / mpc

Navigation of Pop Up Computer is meant to be intuitive. The first screen features a closed book over which users must drag their pointer until it changes into a hand. With this hand icon, the **book** can be opened and pages turned until the contents page — the first pop up spread — is reached. This spread features all twenty-six letters of the alphabet and by clicking on a particular letter, users can be transported to the letter's corresponding spread (e.g. 'A' for Apollo). There is also the option to continue leafing through the book by turning its pages. Clicking on the red marker ribbon at the bottom of the book brings you back to the contents page from anywhere in the book.

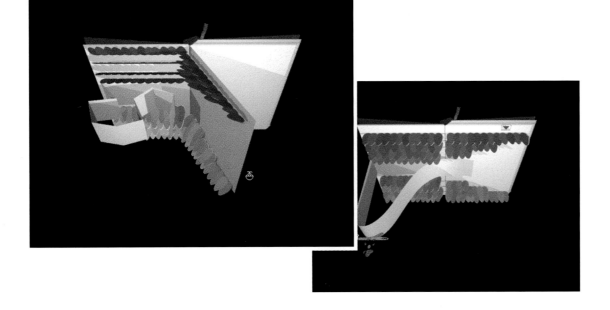

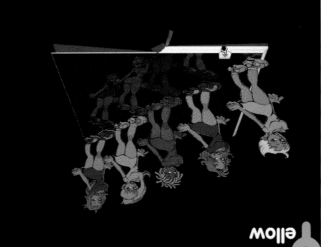

Yellow

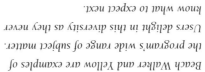

Beach Walker and Yellow are examples of the program's wide range of subject matter. Users delight in this diversity as they never know what to expect next.

Beach Walker

Reality becomes twice removed — democratically, that is — as users are given the occasion to play with virtual fonts on virtual Mac and take an IQ test on a PC.

Navigation within the individual spreads is sometimes more complex. Clicking on an arrow at the bottom of the left–hand page launches and closes each event or **interactive** opportunity. Depending on the nature of the spread's contents — their variety is almost absurd as they range from a space shuttle launch to an IQ test given on a PC — the user may just sit back and witness an event, engage in a test of skill or play at random within the given environment. The presence of the hand icon always indicates that there is something to be done.

Pop Up Computer's success as an interactive experience hinges on its compelling graphics. Everything from **paper texture** and shadows to the mechanics of each spread's unfolding has been flawlessly rendered. The black background gives a sense of three–dimensional presence to the individual spreads. One wonders whether the rather eclectic choice of subject matter was driven by each topic's suitability for visual representation.

Pop Up Computer might easily be classified as an interactive game, were it not for the program's exceptional variety. It might almost be considered a prototype for experimenting with graphically structured interactive opportunities. These opportunities are richly composed to both challenge and entertain the user.

MELISSA DALLAL

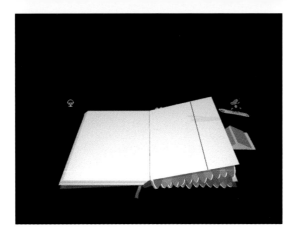

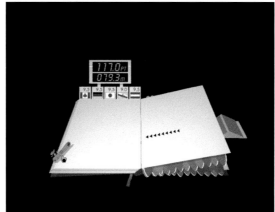

In a test of snowboarding skill, users must direct the angle at which the monkey jumps from the edge of the ramp. If the jump is successful, the monkey soars over the edge of the page which then flips over as he continues his flight. As soon as the monkey lands, his score is posted.

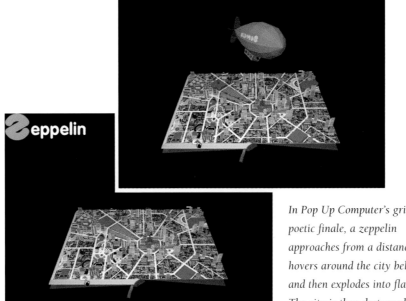

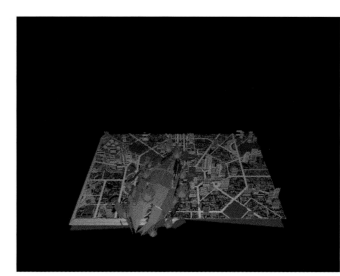

In Pop Up Computer's grim yet poetic finale, a zeppelin approaches from a distance, hovers around the city below and then explodes into flames. The city is then destroyed by fire, and the user is automatically exited from the program.

Magazines

Leafing through the pages of a magazine is a pleasure all its own. The feel, the sound of it, the images flashing by, the fragments of text — everything helps to create a state of effortless concentration. A magazine is an easy way out of this world. It is a convenient way in, as well — it samples the world for the reader. By virtue of this sampling, print magazines can be considered as hypertext *avant la lettre:* the string of articles is not necessarily linear and each article has its own hierarchy of headlines, headers, introduction, text, quotes, cadres, cross–references, etcetera. Standard signs of this highly developed format become signals in multimedia: the click is heard as flipping a page, there are headlines and introductions, now made audible...

The CD–ROM magazine is a hybrid of print and television that combines the qualities and flaws of both. Like TV, it is image–oriented, with the text serving for the most part as link between images. But the images can move; not only can you read the interview, you can see and hear it as well. And it has the flexibility of a print magazine, as it is browsable. A very clear interface containing the hierarchy of the different layers of information is therefore essential to the design of multimedia magazines. The complete range of new graphic signs in multimedia — pictograms, highlighting conventions, utilities like boxes and pop–up screens, lines, colours and noises – is deployed to facilitate the readers' rapid movement within the magazine. Most of these have been developed from existing graphic codes, but interestingly, a lot of the new graphic conventions find their way back to print magazines, stressing the 'hypertext' quality of the 2D format!

It is a fast medium, so a lot of creativity goes into masking the loading time for movies and sound clips: too much watching of static screens would drive readers back to print and TV. So something is moving all the time and there is music in the background. In the design of multimedia magazines, animation retains its full double meaning.

A magazine is an editorial medium. It has a point of view from which it selects and orders information. A clear sign of this point of view is a consistent design policy. A magazine, whether in print or in multimedia, has to have a face, an identity that stands out amidst its competitors. Graphic design for magazines has to do a lot more than functionally order information. As the saying goes about newspapers: The journal is a gentleman.

MAX BRUINSMA

109

ahol a kurzor
mutatóujjá alakul
ott kattintson

INTERAKTÍV MAGAZIN

pc90

1995
II. évfolyam 1. szám

09:32

ABCD Digizine / ABCD Studio

Contents with live preview at upper right.

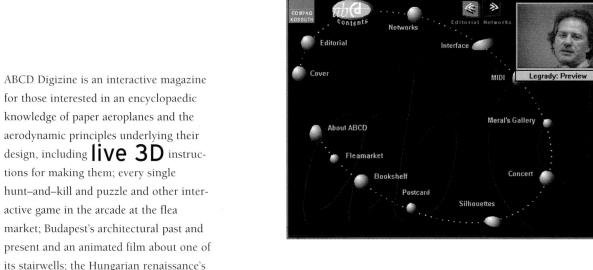

Editorial page. With our help, the editor can occasionally shake his head while asking: am I doing this or you? Or maybe the both of us?

ABCD Digizine is an interactive magazine for those interested in an encyclopaedic knowledge of paper aeroplanes and the aerodynamic principles underlying their design, including **live 3D** instructions for making them; every single hunt–and–kill and puzzle and other interactive game in the arcade at the flea market; Budapest's architectural past and present and an animated film about one of its stairwells; the Hungarian renaissance's origins in Visegrad, including recommended reading (the complete works of Shakespeare with hyperlinks and other functions close at hand); the medium of radio; the most impressive graffiti from around the world; explanatory advertisements of the major providers of technology for the new media; music videos; the vicissitudes of musicians who simply couldn't pay a band and therefore were forced to use machines instead; editorials about all of the aforementioned and much more; an illustrated **catalogue** of genuine, live recordings of English children singing Do You Know the Muffin

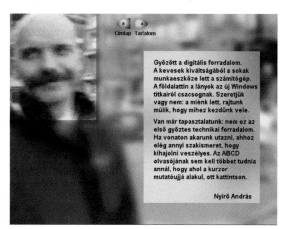

111

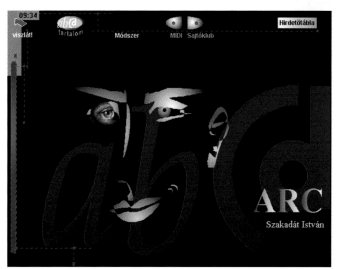

One of the title pages of the regular features. Human eye in drawing opens the contents.

Year of publication 1994 / 1995 **Author** ABCD Studio **Place of publication** Budapest, Hungary **Publisher** IDG Hungary **Copyright owners** ABCD Studio **Design company** ABCD Studio
Screen design Meral Yasar **Animation / graphics** ABCD Studio **Interaction design** I. Szakadát, A. Nyírö, M. Yasar **Sound design** I. Szakadát, A. Nyírö, M. Yasar, G. Kelemen, I. Barczi, G. Gerénnyi
Production ABCD Studio **Editors** I. Szakadát, A. Nyírö, M. Yasar, G. Kelemen, I. Barczi, G. Gerénnyi **Contributors** A. Haradja, L. Turi **Software used** V **Platform** mpc

Article about the Personal Digital Assistant. The different icons produce texts about various aspects of the PDA, including a historical overview.

An interactive postcard of a square in Budapest contains the square's architectural past and present, including the buildings as they were, are and are no more.

Man? and hundreds of other classic children's rhymes while they create all of the sound effects with their own hands and feet; images and samples from a concert by the Balanescu quartet; Manet's Olympia and the world from which it emerged, illuminated by texts of Zola and Mallarmé, with music by Saint–Saëns; how the screen looks backwards; what the names of the streets used to be everywhere before, during and after the revolutions, engaging learned people in a world wide web of discussion about all of the above...in a word, all those interested in culture — those are the 'readers' who will be in **seventh heaven** as they leaf through the screens of ABCD Digizine digital periodical.

The performer in the music video at left explains the how and why of his work in the window at right.

Two of the experiences contained by the postcard. On the left, Istvan Orosz's animated film gives a vivid impression of life in these dwellings, seen through the eyes of a ten–year–old boy in a stairwell. And, last but not least: the cobblestones themselves.

One of the sources of information about the painting contained in the interactive panel at its base: an erudite explanation of the Paris in which it was created in 1866.

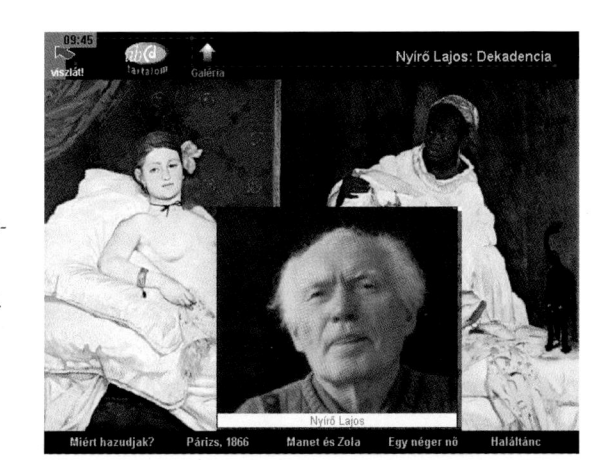

Another part of the concert section. The dots on the violin produce visual images and samples from the quartet's performances.

One enters the contents in the form of a screen with a circular pattern of **spheres** representing the standard categories of Digizine: Bookshelf, MIDI, Flea Market, Postcard, Silhouette, Networks, Meral's Gallery, Cover and Editorial, among others. The first page contains the only instructions really needed to explore this interactive magazine: click where the cursor turns into a hand. The rest is a straightforward hierarchy of hyperlinked texts and other materials with a double icon for moving back and forth between the categories.

Viewers with a genuine interest in culture will probably remember their despair in the past, when confronted with the infantile, dictatorial, **manipulative,** aggressive, monotonous content of television. They can now get a look at what will hopefully soon make such TV obsolete: a form that with enough faith in its viewers to offer astonishing variety and complete control.

Let us hope that this becomes a model and a standard!

JAMES BOEKBINDER

A click produces ghost names of the streets.

The title page of the concert section.

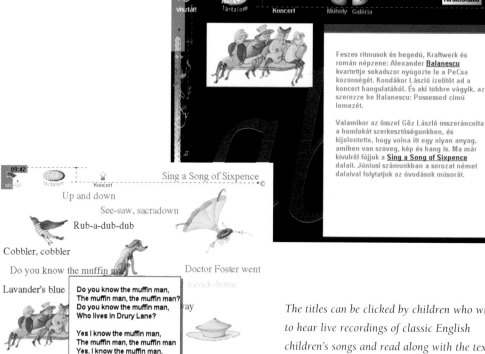

The titles can be clicked by children who wish to hear live recordings of classic English children's songs and read along with the text. The drawings change when clicked.

113

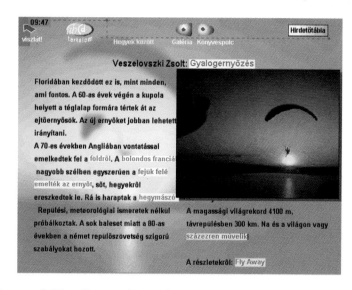

Moving images of gliders illustrate this article.

YOU MY FRIEND HAVE
ACCESSED THE FATAL
DEATH TRAP!

YOUR ASSIGNMENT:
WITHDRAW $80.00
FROM THE AUTOMATIC
TELLER MACHINE FROM HELL!

OR RESTART YOUR COMPUTER!!!

24 HOUR BANKING
VIRTUAL CREDIT
THE THIRD INTERNATIONAL BANK OF

* 0 #
7 8 9
4 5 6
1 2 3

Blender / Dennis International

Billed as an interactive pop culture magazine, Blender densely packs exciting graphics, video, audio and text into a standard magazine format, supplying its own breed of digital entertainment on CD–ROM. Its contents are made up of celebrity profiles, feature articles and regular departments that include music, film and game reviews, a fashion column, horoscopes, a **digital art** gallery and a comic strip. While these venues are rooted in the conventions of the print idiom, their structure allows for easy navigation and accommodates the use of more unorthodox and inventive interfaces.

Organised in a conventional magazine format, Blender features a lively table of contents whose strobing globes provide access to its various departments. Dragging the cursor over the screen reveals text bubbles that indicate the focus of each department, while clicking on the screen's centre, which reads Map, displays a breakdown of topics covered. Clicking directly on one of the departments reveals a more graphically informative sub–menu.

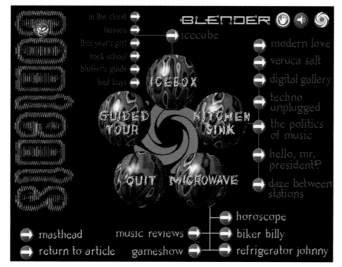

All of Blender's destinations are clearly mapped out according to various sub–menus that can be accessed throughout the CD. In addition to previewing, these menus prolong the journey to particular information, so that users can **enjoy** more graphically elaborate sequences. Arrows and page number charts allow users to move readily back and forth within individual sequences, while clicking on the Blender logo at top right takes the user back to the main menu.

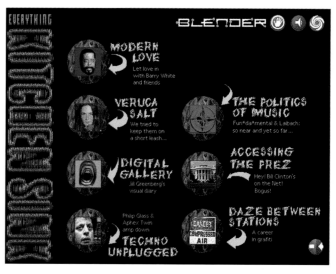

Year of publication 1994 **Author** Dennis International **Place of publication** New York, USA **Publisher** Jenny von Feldt **Copyright owners** Felix Dennis **Awards** ID Magazine '95

Design company Dennis International **Screen design** Jason Pearson **Animation / graphics** Shawn Belshwender **Interaction design** David Cherry **Sound design** Tony Cruz

Production David Cherry, Jason Pearson **Editor** Howard Stringer **Contributors** Dan Catalano, Paula Bernstein, Tom Semiljan, June Joseph **Software used** APS, QXP, AI, APR, MMD, SD **Platform** mac / mpc

Hyperactive yet seamlessly orchestrated text and graphics, in conjunction with a straightforward navigational system, cultivate an addictive pace at which users are meant to move through the CD. As words and images flash, strobe and travel across the screen accompanied by **ambient** loops of music, a heightened sense of excitement is created. The use of vibrant colours also adds allure to each screen's lavish interface. Highlighted text or an inset video screen indicates when there is an opportunity to access supplementary information, whether in the form of text, image or video.

Unexpected elements are also woven throughout Blender. At random moments, clicking on a word will trigger a **trap door** to open and take users to an otherwise inaccessible zone of the CD. Advertisements appear on a similarly unexpected basis. As users move back and forth between different departments, ads pop up. But users always have the option to explore or ignore them.

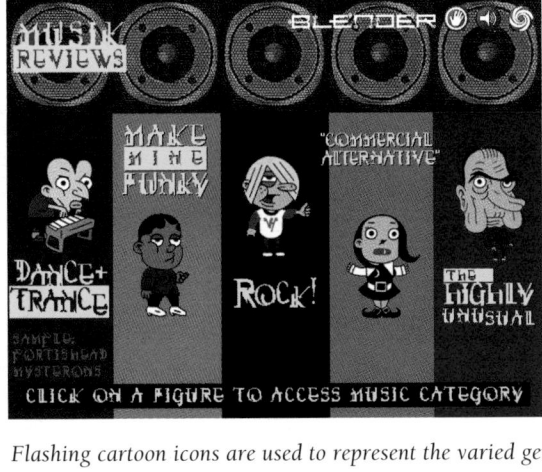

Flashing cartoon icons are used to represent the varied genres within Blender's music review section. Like most of Blender's interfaces, clicking on one of the characters reveals a sub–menu from which users can access a selection of albums and then from there access specific reviews, music samples and video clips.

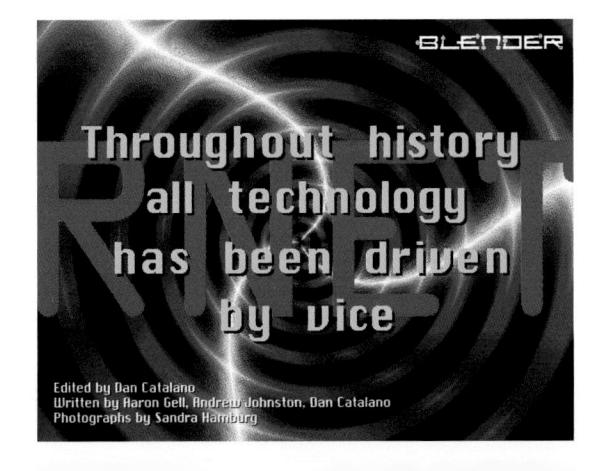

By clicking on one of the signs on the spinning zodiac wheel, users can access their horoscope, which in each issue is read by a different celebrity.

Another unpredictable element within the CD is the death–trap. Those unable to resist the temptation of the unknown click the skull on the main menu and are transported to a frustratingly inescapable area where they are **tormented** by the sound of nails scraping a blackboard or an ATM from which it is impossible to withdraw cash. In these cases a force quit is the only option for escape. Yet, if the user has not exhausted the over six hour's worth of Blender's material, even a run–in with the death–trap will not deter them from coming back for more.

MELISSA DALLAL

Blender's main features are packed with video clips, side bars and, as always, flashing, spinning and moving graphics and text. Here, a feature on the Internet simulates the experience of being on–line and downloading pornography.

117

Blender's digital art gallery and fashion column are featured regularly under the Fixtures department.

Members:
What's New
Your View
Forgot Password?

Nonmembers:
Overview
Why Be a Member?
Join!

HOTWIRED

Tom-Tom Club

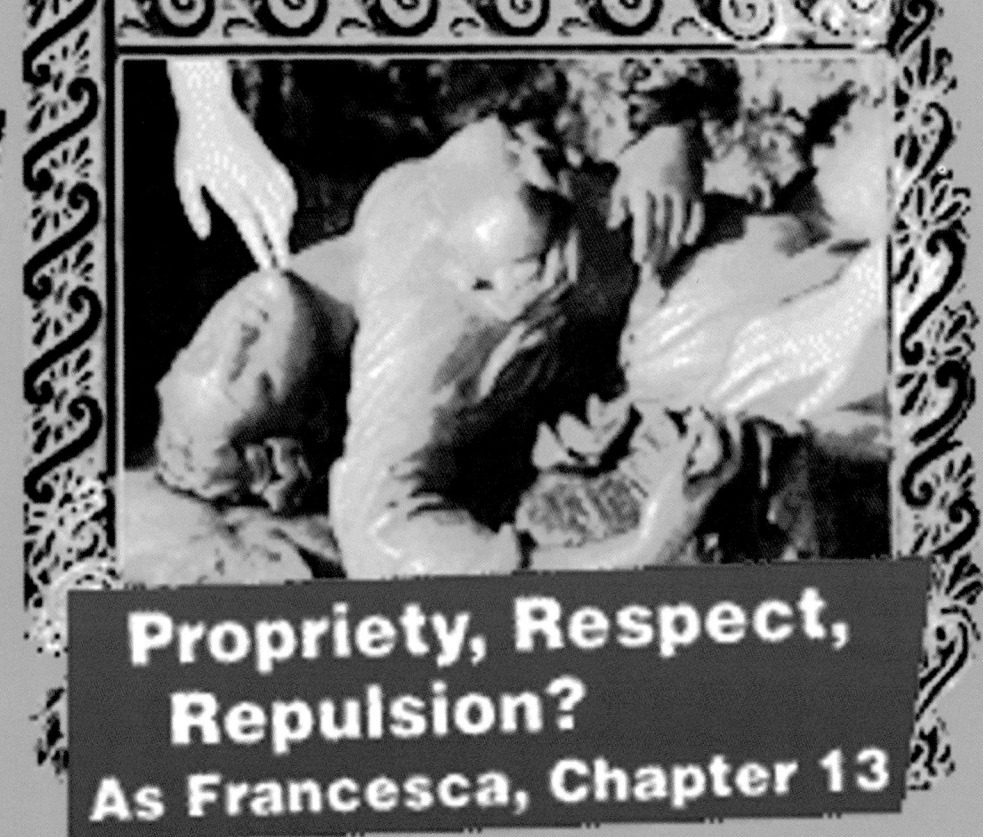

Propriety, Respect, Repulsion?
As Francesca, Chapter 13

James Morrow
Tuesday,

Club Wired

HotWired / HotWired Ventures L.L.C.

Overview, with updated list of features for each section of the site and access to new features or feedback pages.

Wired magazine's web site retains many of the qualities of its printed counterpart. It has the same editorial strengths and bright graphic style, but with the additional fresh qualities of **live information** and discussion afforded by the Internet. A traditional magazine could never hope to encompass as much as this well–orchestrated site.

The initial task for the first–time user is to register with HotWired for the princely sum of some personal information: your e–mail address. The general layout of information is comprehensive, with plenty of help and search functions to keep even the most timid 'net–surfer' happy. Once you are onto the introductory content pages, you are aware that you have entered a very vibrant electronic domain. There is a wide selection of articles and topic areas to explore. You only wish that your computer could instantaneously dispense a coffee, a **doughnut** and some ambient chatter while your browse through the material on offer.

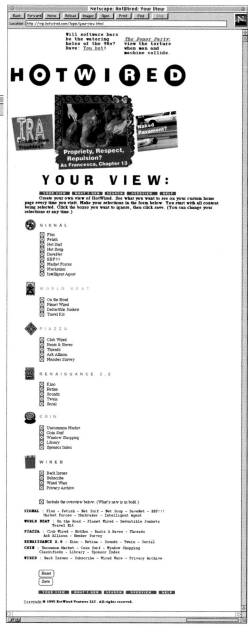

119

Year of publication 1995 **Author** HotWired Ventures L.L.C. **Place of publication** http://www.hotwired.com **Publisher** HotWired Ventures L.L.C.

Copyright owners HotWired Ventures L.L.C. **Awards** Digital Hollywood '95, Computer Press Awards '95, National Information Infrastructure Awards '95

Design company HotWired Ventures L.L.C. **Screen design** Barbara Kuhr, John Plunkett, Max Kisman, Jeffrey Veen, Sabine Messner

Production Carl Steadman, Jill Atkinson **Editors** Louis Rossetto, Chip Bayers, Gary Wolf, June Cohen, John Alderman, Julie Petersen, Susanna Camp **President** Andrew Anker **Platform** www

In HotWired's unguided tour, you are presented with a mission statement that they are a station on the World Wide Web with five channels offering access to the latest aspects of the digital revolution. Continuing with this metaphor, HotWired TV's Signal channel offers news and reviews on information technology.

In this site, the emphasis is on the delivery of a rich collection of writing together with the access to forums of discussion and debate. The graphic style has a fast and **furious** quality, with a tumultuous collection of randomly textured and brightly coloured backgrounds. You will find everything from flat fields of lurid green to swathes of pale pastels behind the caption blocks and body copy. To complete the spectrum, various articles and function windows (such as search and registration) are set against standard grey.

World Beat, the travel channel, contains elaborately illustrated articles with cunningly incorporated advertising. In these particular examples you can see 'Zima Clearmalt' and 'Saturn' adverts which effectively coax the viewer into accessing more information about the products.

You can rant and rave in a more restrained environment (in this case, accompanied by an eye-catching Motorola advert).

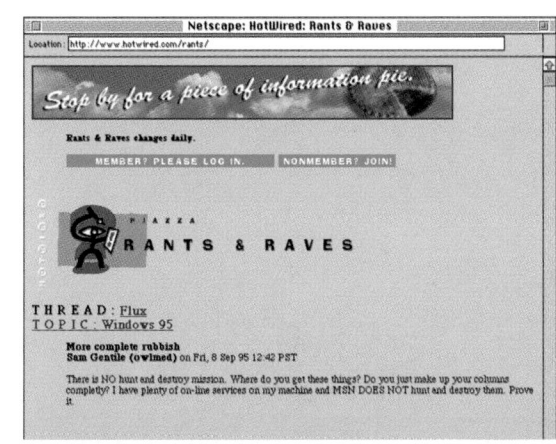

The Piazza section acts as an electronic forum of discussion. You can have your intelligent questions answered by 'Allison' in her kitsch boudoir.

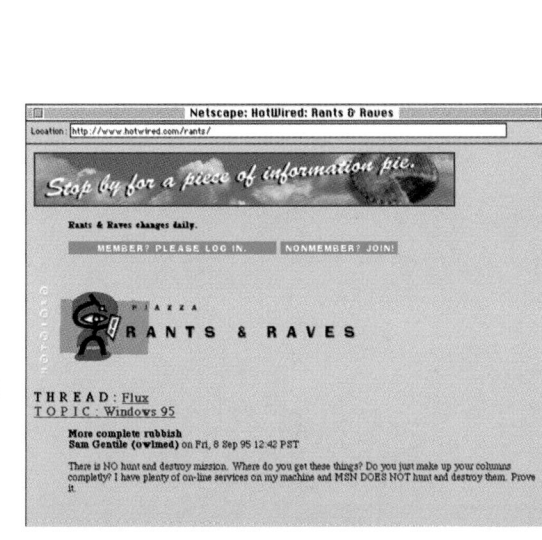

Each section of the content is represented by its own distinctive icon. The identity and contents of each are clearly colour–coded and listed in the overview. As you enter each section, the relevant channel identity stays at the head of the page, so you are always aware of your location. Many pages contain adverts, which are surprisingly unobtrusive, as they are incorporated within the page layouts in the same space as the title captions. Some of the most interesting areas of the site are the discussion pages. Club Wired and the Threads pages allow you to link to **live** Internet conversations and retrieve old ones. Threads is described as the place to hang out for good company and lively conversation…all you need are some real people!

The HotWired site is a lively and logical extension of Wired in print. When you consider all the added values of it being on the Internet, you wonder how long it will remain on paper.

GILES ROLLESTONE

Renaissance 2.0 , 'the arts channel'. In the arts section, screen designs vary from the bold coloration and layout of the Retina lead feature to the subtler approach of the illustrated Nude–Not Lewd article and Gallery space where the background textures closely reflect the editorial updates.

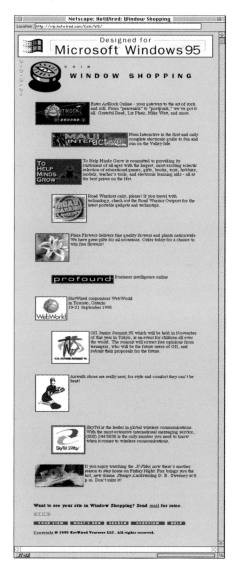

121

Coin is a section for digital home shopping and access to Wired's library, just one of the many bold, modular designs throughout the site which allows for frequent editorial updates.

Mercury Communications

The Mercury campaign has developed considerable rapport with the younger audience

Ruddles

Maynard's

Fruitella

Midland

1   6

Informer One / Studio Dm, Colin Taylor, Jonathan Taylor

The Informer CD–ROM is released bi–annually and its function is to provide market research for advertising agencies. This is not perhaps the most inspiring brief for a digital publication, but the interactive design by London–based Studio DM has created a startlingly fresh way of communicating the state of the marketplace. The disc represents a **radical** departure from the usual dry documentation that communicates such information to the moguls of the advertising industry. Informer is literally unique, in that every issue is specific to its consumer. Unlike most CD–ROMs, Informer is designed for a rarefied audience. Companies pay an annual subscription fee for access to the marketing data contained in each issue.

Issue One has a wealth of video clips showing candid interviews and discussions with young people in which views on existing advertising are explored. The net effect is of an audio–visual encyclopaedia of opinion that conveys a general picture of the range of individuals within specific consumer groups.

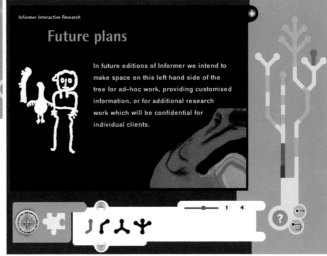

By way of introduction, Informer's mission statement is framed within its thematic context. The disc is one of a series — information regarding subsequent issues is provided.

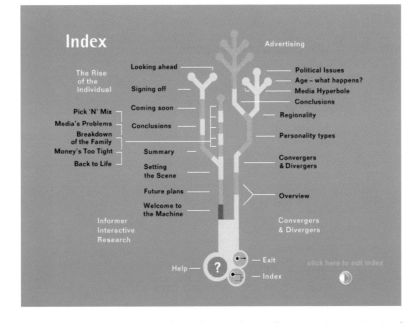

The hidden superstructure of the navigational tree is clearly illustrated. This exploded view shows the amount of information that is neatly condensed into its purely symbolic counterpart. In this issue, the content is divided into three themed sections — Convergers and Divergers, The Rise of the Individual and Advertising.

Year of publication 1994 **Author** Studio Dm; Colin Taylor; Jonathan Taylor **Place of publication** London, UK **Publisher** Informer Interactive Research Ltd.
Copyright owners Studio Dm **Design company** Studio Dm, Colin Taylor, Jonathan Taylor **Screen design** Studio Dm **Animation / graphics** Studio Dm **Interaction design** Studio Dm
Sound design Jonathan Taylor, Studio Dm **Production** Studio Dm **Editors** Informer Interactive **Software used** SC, DD, RSG, MT, AVS, PPP **Platform** mac

When the user clicks on the small plus icon in the middle of the screen, a profiles panel opens. The function of this section is to provide profiles on the young people featured in the video sequences.

In this debut issue, the graphic language is as strong as some of the verbal expletives to be found in the youthful interviews. The undeniable emphasis on 'singing stained glass' colours reflects the developers' concern with the creation of an application that is at once lively and easy to use. To this end, a navigational tree is constantly at hand, providing a bold, clear map of your journey through the material. Each issue of the Informer series addresses four different topics which may, for example, range from the influence of gay culture on advertising to regional stereotypes. The structure of the content is reflected by the colour–coded segments of the **nodal tree** on the right–hand side of the screen. When you have selected and browsed through a section of the content, its respective segment on the tree darkens in colour (it simply leaves an interactive trail).

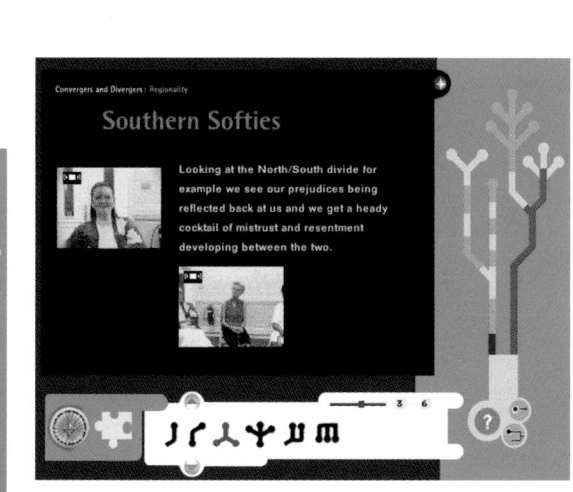

Studio Dm developed a branching tree' or route map metaphor that indicates the user's position in the application and the sections that have already been viewed. The panel at the base of the screen displays the additional nodes of information available within each segment of the tree. In the Convergers and Divergers section of the disc, the impact of regional stereotyping and its effect on advertising is boldly illustrated.

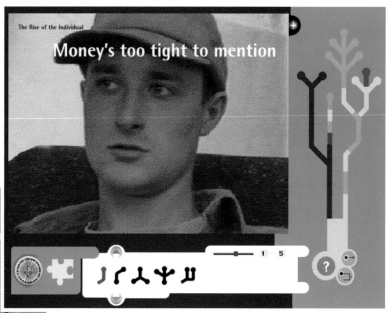

The interface design has a playful as well as practical character. A spin on the roulette icon and you are randomly jettisoned into a different section of the disc. Another lively feature is the many typographical animations included with the video material. In some instances, written words fall into sync with audio clips of colloquial speech, strongly enhancing their illustrative effect.

The fundamental strength of Informer is its **structure,** which has been designed from the outset to provide a flexible framework to allow for changes in content from issue to issue. Studio DM has its roots in digital typography, and along with the disc's other emphatically unique qualities, a collection of live screen fonts were specially created for the project.

GILES ROLLESTONE

The advertising section focuses on young people's responses to television advertising and marketing campaigns, providing regular, consumer–based research for advertising agencies, marketing agencies, media companies and product developers.

Sans ... ...tre monde ne serait qu'une vallée de larmes.

...'abord cru à sa folie

...évélé poète *brazil...*

avec des ... ...himères

...utop... ...ser

de nos ca...

contre la...

de répi... ...cer un ... ...et

int... ...et par la meill...

un CDROM ...

Totale Perte de Temps...

La Vague Interactive / LVI Presse, Sylvain Roume

La Vague's playful logo, an intriguing graphic monogram, cleverly constructed out of sound file preview icons.

The La Vague Interactive CD–ROM magazine intrigues you even before you've opened the main application. In the first window, you find a **reptile** lolling on a blue Stetson, seamlessly constructed from a patchwork of preview icons. Double–click on any portion of this graphic motif and you hear animal noises and musical extracts — an enticing start to your interactive journey.

Unusually, when you launch the magazine, a whole screen is dedicated to displaying your computer's compatibility with the requirements of the CD–ROM. Data about installed system software and other technical issues flow into a **humorous layout** with a Humphrey Bogart couple as its centrepiece. Next, you make the acquaintance of a miniature Muybridge figure who runs off into the darkness, leading you into the main body of the content. The same diminutive figure stays with you throughout, charged with the task of performing various acrobatics at appropriate moment as you travel between sections.

You can select an item either from the layered headings in the main content menu or from the Hypernavigator. The latter actually tracks your movements and acts as a record of your journey through the disc.

127

Year of publication 1994 **Author** LVI Presse, Sylvain Roume **Place of publication** Paris, France **Publisher** Les Éditions Numériques **Copyright owners** LVI Presse, Les Éditions Numériques

Awards 'Sum Mac' Magazine's: Best cd-rom of the year '94, Möbius Special Prize '94 (under the auspices of CNRS & UNESCO) **Design company** LVI-Presse **Screen design** Nicolas Thépot **Animation / graphics** Nicolas Thépot, Gilles Iltis

Interaction design Jean-Luc Lamarque **Sound design** Stéphane Garin **Production** Thierry Keller **Editor** Michel Besnier **Contributors** "Too many to mention" **Software** Yves Ada **Platform** mac / mpc

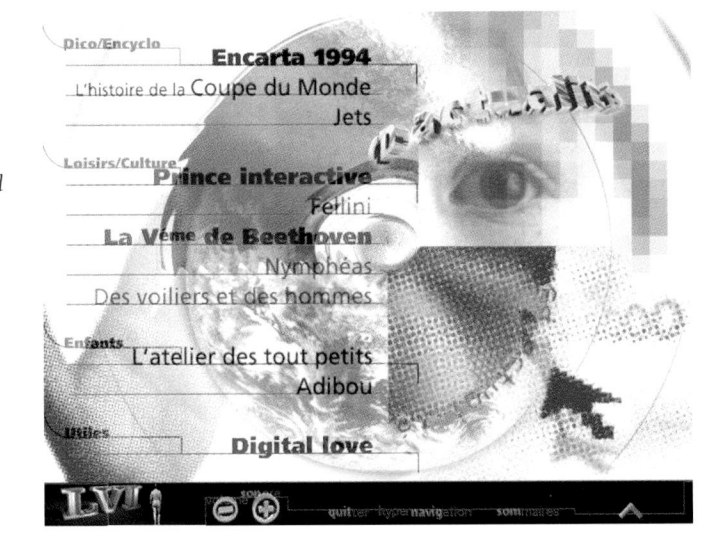

The top level of the CD publications reviews section has a cleverly integrated design incorporating menu items layered over a carefully constructed illustration based on a CD.

The striking thing about this work is its cleanly conceived interactive structure and elegant graphic design. La Vague Interactive has a thoroughly integrated navigational system, which outdoes itself in its attempt to make content accessible. The delicately rendered controls stretching across the bottom of the screen further enhance the sense of **transparency** and fluidity of movement. This infinitely controllable environment is achieved with the help of captions which continuously prompt your actions: you are instantly informed whenever your cursor rolls over any potential access point.

All this empirical rigour gives way without protest to a light–hearted **atmosphere** and a selection of articles ranging from a look at the future of television to a collection of informative Letters from Mongolia. This would seem an unlikely mixture at first, but each section of this work glides effortlessly into the next, making such polarities insignificant.

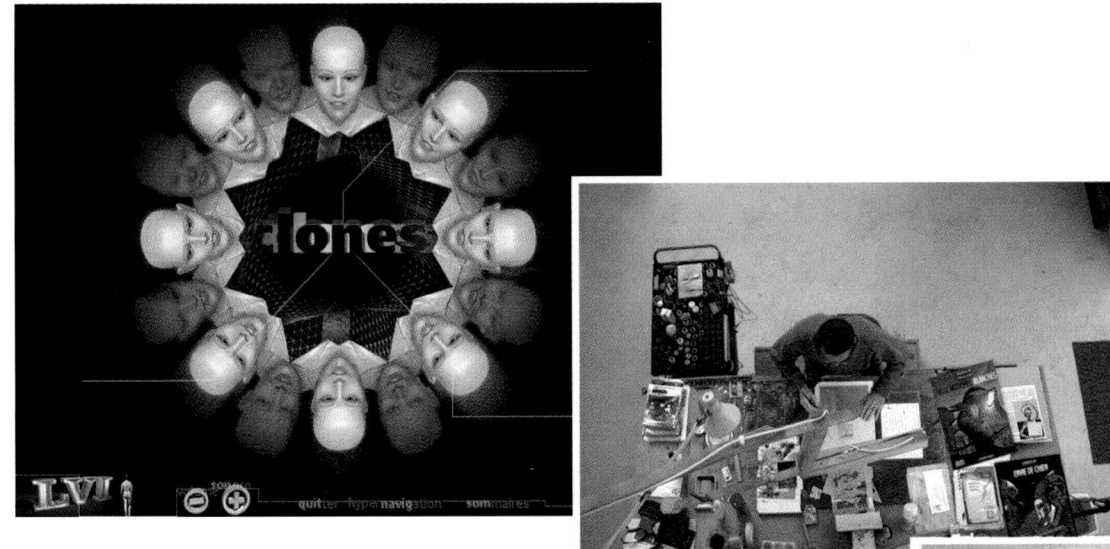

The magazine is divided into six themed sections, with ten illustrated and animated articles, all cleanly crafted with atmospheric digital illustration and typography. Viewing a representative screen from each area, from CD–ROM reviews to the Kids Planet, you can see how each screen design is sympathetic to its subject matter.

Almost every section of this disc surprises and inspires you with some unique attribute. The obligatory titles reviews are done with enough imagination and variety to stimulate even the most jaded CD–ROM consumer. The visual styling varies in order to best illustrate the individual qualities of each subject. One set of reviews is characterised by a digital illustration style akin to April Greiman, while another is introduced with a full–-screen Monty Python extravaganza. Arguably the most evocative sequence of screen layouts is to be found in the section about **Mongolia.** For just a moment, the intricate sequence of collaged stills and native music gives you a glimpse of another world.

GILES ROLLESTONE

Tomorrow's Television Today, a playful article in which you control the arm of the ultimate couch–potato — just one click for instant gratification.

129

On the Kids Planet, you are transported once again into an immersive environment where an enchanting animated story unfolds, replete with customised kiddie controllers at the base of the screen.

bomb the bass clear

NME

DARK HEART

UnZip / IPC Magazines, Zone (UK)

The Intersection provides an atmospheric arena in which to explore aspects of global graphics street language. Click on a poster on one wall and you open a montaged comic book with angular windows containing sampled clips of Japanese animation and pulsating captions.

Open UnZip and you enter a multifaceted head–space, densely packed with **consumer culture** imagery set in an urban jungle atmosphere. The disc features a gallery space called Altar State, a media space entitled Checkpoint, an Internet data space or Netropolis, a Music Documentary section, a street culture Intersection, and a Pleasuredrome.

131

From the start, you are presented with The Head – the central metaphor and navigational device which guides you through the content. The Head is your host , a bald, anonymous individual with six symbols engraved on his scalp. He is your gateway into each themed zone. Click on a symbol and a panel of the cranium caves in with a resounding 'squelch'. Once you have made your initial selection, The Head's counterpart, his 'alter ego', appears surrounded by symbols on bright spherical satellites. Rollover the 'alter ego' head and the satellites scintillate; tug his ear and you control the sound levels; select a satellite and you enter one of the six themed sections of the disc.

Year of publication 1995 Author IPC Magazines, Zone (UK) Place of publication London, UK Publisher Zone UK Ltd., IPC Magazines Ltd. Copyright owners Zone UK Ltd., IPC Magazines Ltd.

Design company Zone UK Ltd., IPC Magazines Ltd. Screen design Ken Frakes, Raja Choudhury, Mudimo Okondo, Kirk Goble, Emma Westecott Animation / graphics Kirk Goble, Raja Choudhury, Mudimo Okondo, Emma Westecott

Interaction design Ken Frakes, Raja Choudhury, Mudimo Okondo, Kirk Goble, Emma Westecott Sound design Chris Blanchard Production Zone UK Ltd. Editors Ken Frakes @ Zone UK Ltd., Lolin Tough @ IPC Magazines Ltd.

Contributors Kak, Lisa Verico, Charles Arthur, David Taylor, Nick Wray, David O'Higgins Software used APS, SSP, APR, MMD Platform mac / mpc

The overall visual style is as bold as it is eclectic with striking and well-recorded sounds throughout. Each thematic environment has its own specific and evocative quality, whether 'Gothic—digital,' as in the aspiring temple wall displaying **graffiti** in a section of the Altar State gallery, or high corporate kitsch in the CheckPoint area sponsored by VOX. Throughout the disc, the emphasis is on physical and spatial illustration. Quirky, tactile objects house the content and slickly produced, confidently animated devices drive the user from section to section. Textual information, when it emerges, is in a hectic array of styles ranging from the unique and autographic in the Intersection environment to the unassuming sans serif in Netropolis.

The origins of the six thematic symbols used in the central navigational device are described at length in the gallery section. In-depth information about specific graphic **symbols** is a rare find and it is endearing to share such reverence for symbolic minutiae, however contrived.

Checkpoint zone.

The Technicolor labyrinth allows access to a collection of art work, some visceral animated sequences and much more...

Altar State zone, Sick's Gallery.

Intersect zone, Technofear feature.

You learn about the Internet in a padded blue room. Its surreal furniture leads you to gems of wisdom that appear on sliding **blue tablets** looming like soft upholstery in the private space. In stark contrast, Intersection confronts you with a gritty, graffiti–laden back street. Roll over the writing on the wall and an imaginatively animated sequence brings you to statements concerning global youth culture.

In the gallery space, the contrasts continue. Brief, biographical detail with pensive, figurative works by David Scheinmann in one segment and the gloriously twisted and visceral Polythene Jon Show by David O Higgins in the next...radically different ends of the visual communication spectrum, all in one equally polytheistic environment.

The graphical atmosphere in the Music Documentary section featuring Bomb the Bass is different again, with an ambient approach akin to MTV. Zone (UK) Limited, UnZip's producers, are well versed in this genre. This is clearly demonstrated by their **touch-screen** 'VidZone' systems installed in both HMV and Tower Records in London. UnZip is also featured on–line, as part of Zone's continuing bid to provide popular media for an increasingly fragmented youth culture.

GILES ROLLESTONE

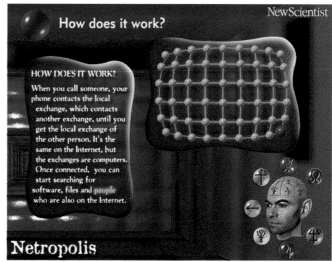

Netropolis zone — How the Internet works article.

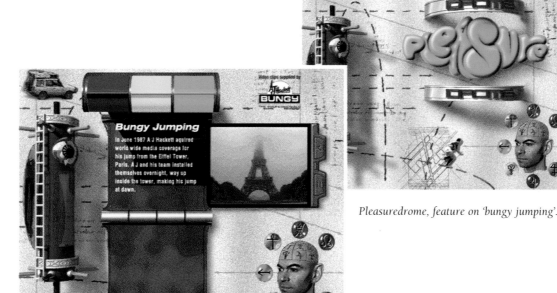

Pleasuredrome, feature on 'bungy jumping'.

Le Cri Néerlandais, Opéra, 1995

Promotional

Designers of promotional web sites or CD–ROMs face an awkward problem: they want to dictate their viewers' input, but must simultaneously try to simulate at least a minimum of interactivity. The keyword here is choice. You mash up your client's message into as many pieces as possible and there they are: choices, displayed on a background that says it all! Tightly linked to lead to the inevitable 'look what we've done for you!'

A promotional web site offers hitherto unheard–of possibilities of leading (potential) customers along the shelves of your virtual shopping mall. As in the malls, the design of web sites is very much concerned with enticing the lurker to follow a well–laid–out path that ends at each product (and an e–mail ordering form!) and then leads back again. To the client, promoting their products is serious business. For the customer, it should be entertainment. Extra fun can be built in with links to related sites, games, prices

and nice–to–know information that links the product to a life–style context. But too much hyperlinking can lead the browser astray — one should not lose contact with the client's base. A door must remain wide open, leading back to what it is really all about: look what we've done for you!

Traditionally, promotional activities and advertising suffer from a lack of feedback on effectiveness and public reach. This makes the World Wide Web a place of great potential interest for advertisers: the Web not only offers exact information on 'contact moments', it allows for registering geographical and other data of its visitors and gives room for direct feedback from — and to — the customer. Person–to–person marketing — the wet dream of any marketer! The designers know this, and if they are smart, they will try to use every trick in the book to simulate this person–to–person environment.

Visuality is an end in itself here, because the maker is on view. Their products — be they hardware or software — are only marginally accessible; you can show off, but you cannot give it all away. This causes heavy emphasis to be placed on the design of backgrounds, as they constitute the main visual continuity between the different levels of information. But here, backgrounds and artwork cannot be just informative. They have to serve the age–old goal of any promotional activity: window–dressing.

MAX BRUINSMA

135

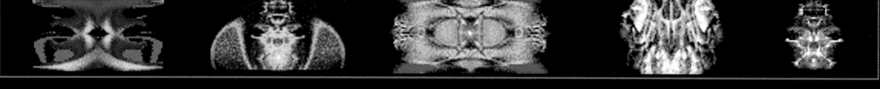

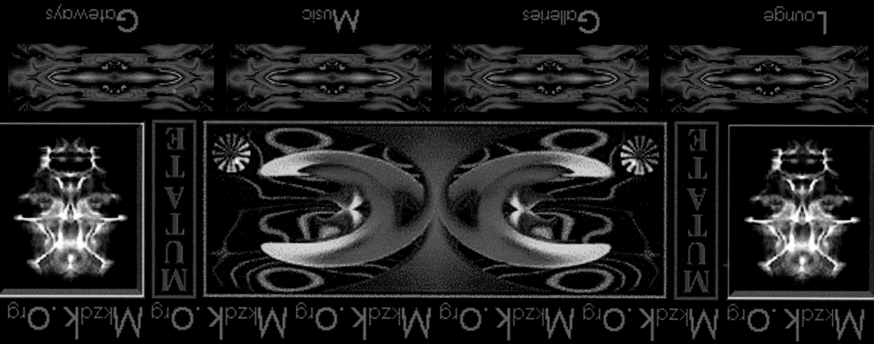

The home area displaying the Sound Machine window that allows the playback of incidental sounds throughout the site. At the bottom of the home area are the graphic identities of each of the three main areas dividing the content.

Surfing the World Wide Web can take up a great deal of your time and patience, and often the rewards are limited. It is refreshing to come across a web site, designed by Michael Samyn/ Zupergraphyx!, that represents a genuine attempt to develop the Internet into an inspiring **visual** experience. More than this, the site offers a compendium of many other sites that share the same dynamic approach to designing for the net.

ISDM (Interactive Study and Documentation on Multimedia) is based in Brussels and is an interactive centre for arts, media and cultural theory. You will not find the standard grey backgrounds and hypertext–only interactivity here. What you find is a series of richly coloured graphic environments with the unusual addition of sound clips played through Sound Machine software (which you need to install on your computer for the full effect).

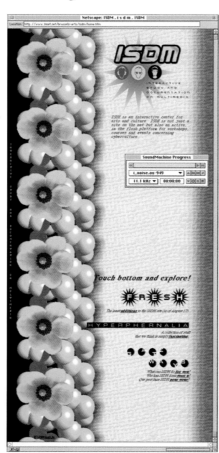

In the lush, velvety green of the Fresh zone, you can access the latest stimulating web sites.

137

Year of publication 1995 **Author** Michael Samyn, Zupergraphyx! **Place of publication** http://www.innet.net/Zupergraphyx! **Publisher** INNET **Copyright owners** Michael Samyn

Design company Zupergraphyx! **Screen design** Zupergraphyx! **Animation / graphics** Zupergraphyx! **Interaction design** Zupergraphyx! **Sound design** Zupergraphyx! **Production** Michael Samyn

Editors Jan Depauw, Michael Samyn **Contributors** Michael Samyn, Veerle Meeussen, Rudy Dewaele, Jan Depauw, Stefaan Quix **Software used** NDE, PR, CD, PSP, PS, GCS, GW **Platform** www

The opening page sets the tone with a poetic phrase that pictures you as a weary **wanderer** in salty cyberwaters, accompanied by the sound of seagulls. One of the first things you notice on the homepage is the prominent ISDM logo, resembling a Sega logo with Designers Republic attitude. From the home area, you can see that the content is divided into three main areas: Fresh, Hyperphernalia and Gateways. Examination reveals these to be three ways of providing the same thing: a window onto a wealth of fascinating work being published on the Internet .

The core screens of each section have impressive, textured backgrounds which are carefully designed so that they can be efficiently rendered in narrow strips. Fresh provides a list of the newest additions to the existing collection of links. Hyperphenalia houses the list of ISDM's favourite creative and expressive **web pages.** Gateways contains more information about the ISDM team and its various activities in World Wide Web and multimedia development, as well as additional links.

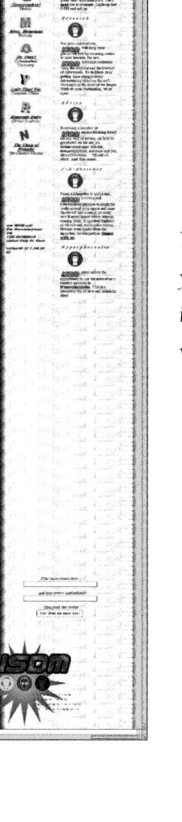

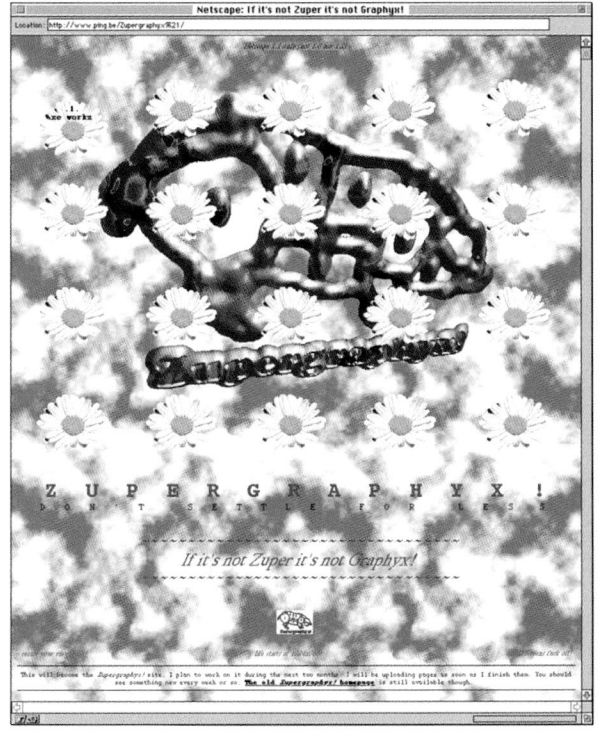

The clean colours and layout of the Gateways screens give you an insight into the activities of the ISDM team, including Zupergraphyx!, the design team responsible for ISDM's visuals. (If it's not Zuper, it's not Graphyx!)

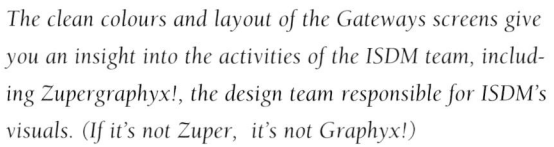

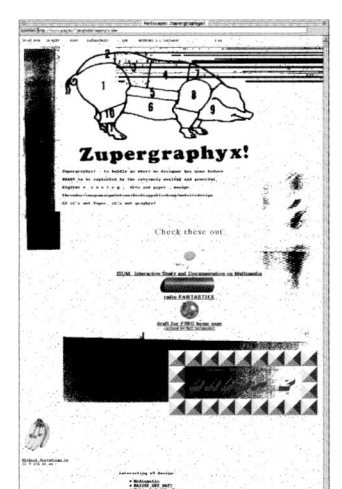

Along with its unique graphics, it is the quality of the linked sites that gives ISDM its character. It would take hundreds of hours of surfing the net to find gems such as animated sequences, **ambient sounds** and a variety of miscellaneous experiments that generally aim at subverting the Netscape status quo.

ISDM represents a bold attempt to overcome the current limitations of the Internet, where most web sites barely exploit existing Internet software capabilities. The site not only explores the medium technically, but adds a spark of graphic sophistication and style to an often visually impoverished Cyberspace.

GILES ROLLESTONE

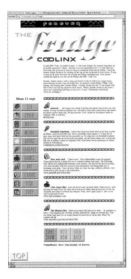

The Exit and Shed screens give you several last chances to go foraging for fascinating web addresses before you leave the site.

The Hyperphenalia opening screen warns that you are ...on the threshold of a mind-blasting experience as you browse through their favourite web pages.

139

Two examples from the wide range of sites linked to ISDM: the Fridge, for a look at what's really cool on the net and MkzdK, as obscure as they come in both name and content.

PLAY
PIA VAN MMELEN

Le Cri Néerlandais : Défilé sans Public
OPERA INTERACTIVE MEDIA

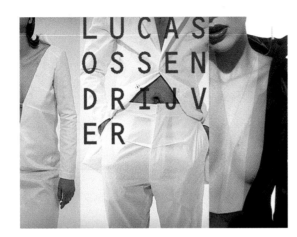

This CD–ROM invites us to view the fashion designs of Pascale Gatzen, Viktor and Rolf, Saskia van Drimmelen, Lucas Ossendrijver and Marcel Verheyen of design group Le Cri Néerlandais.

The movement of the models (and other elements, such as animations of patterns combining to form a design) seems **to balance** on the very edge where 'still' stops and 'moving picture' begins. The space in which the models move has also been reduced to the bare minimum needed to evoke dimensionality. The result is a curious kind of page–like, graphic beauty: the clothes can be examined with the precision with which one examines vivid photographs, while the models move through a careful arrangement of a few poses, sometimes performing a gesture, approaching, turning or receding. They share a main interface of a simple triptych that begins by inviting one to play and make a choice.

The designs of Lucas Ossendrijver. Note paging device at bottom, allowing viewer to leaf through several more pages like this and activate the designs (links are represented by encircled figures).

Lucas Ossendrijver in centre panel.

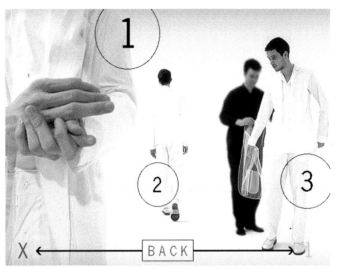

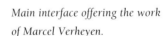

141

Main interface offering the work of Marcel Verheyen.

Year of publication 1995 **Author** Opera Interactive Media, Frans Bevers, René van Binsbergen, Ton Homburg **Place of publication** Amsterdam, Netherlands **Publisher** The Netherlands Design Institute

Copyright owners The Netherlands Design Institute, Opera Interactive Media **Design company** Opera Interactive Media **Screen design** Opera Interactive Media **Animation / graphics** Opera Interactive Media

Interaction design Opera Interactive Media **Sound design** Opera Interactive Media **Production** Opera Interactive Media **Editors** The Netherlands Design Institute, Opera Interactive Media

Contributors Le Cri Néerlandais, Opera Interactive Media, The Netherlands Design Institute **Software used** MMD **Platform** mac / mpc

Marcel Verheyen's designs. Spoken text and links in the form of words that briefly appear on the screen underpin viewer interaction.

A model turns, very close.

One returns to the triptych to make each new choice of a designer. Various links are offered in the form of words **flashed** on the screen. They allow us to influence the arrangement of the movements, or the composition (and sometimes the colour) of the outfits, on beautifully page–like screens.

The presentation of the individual designers is highly original and finely attuned to the character of each. Lucas Ossendrijver's designs are arranged in groups throughout a number of pages, which we flip using a bi–directional arrow at the bottom of the screen, helped by flashing words that inform us of our place in the 'catalogue'.

Looking at a design by Viktor and Rolf. The blue code at lower left is a link to the materials used in the design on view.

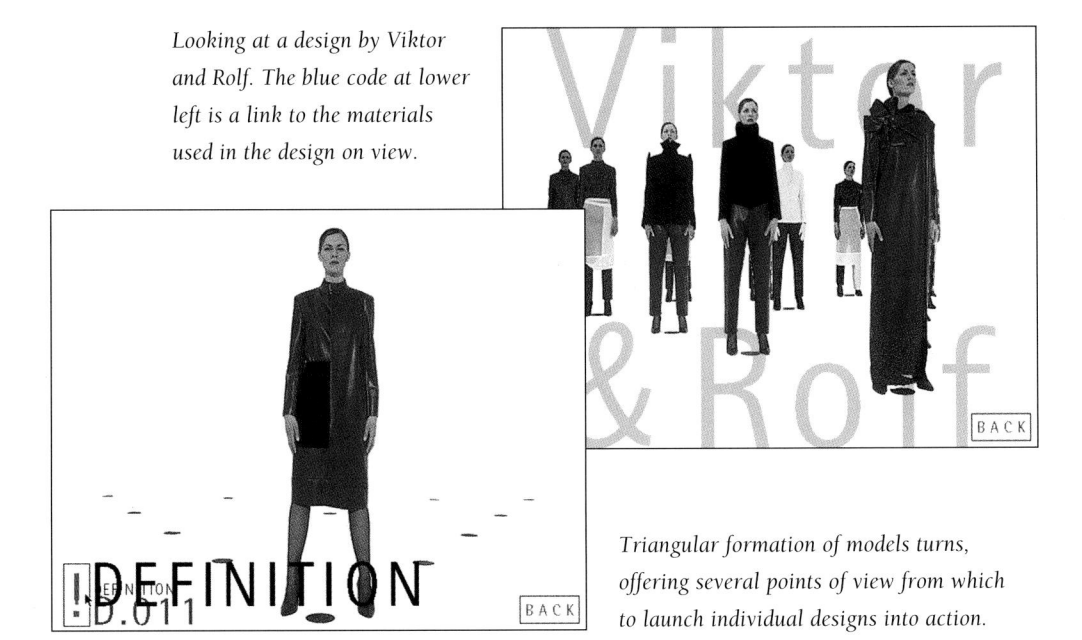

Triangular formation of models turns, offering several points of view from which to launch individual designs into action.

Interface with Pascale Gatzen's work. Five models in motion without leaving the spot.

Modelling a design of Pascale Gatzen, close.

A simple click shows us a new colour scheme.

Marcel Verheyen's designs come at us head on, activated by a panel of eight buttons at left. A voice–over and large visual signals in the form of words (PUSH NOW) spur us on to **intervene** and find out more. A triangular formation of models passes us in revue with the works of Viktor and Rolf. The place markers denoting the triangular field remain while a model shows the individual designs. In the screen offering us work by Pascale Gatzen, five distant figures move without leaving their places in a row. The models showing Saskia van Drimmelen's designs enter and exit the screen like a stage.

The sobriety of this visual design is offset by a rather high tempo (including the tempo with which links are offered and withdrawn), occasionally underpinned by fragments of music or spoken texts. The viewer has only to fall into (or out of) step and lose themselves in the movable **visual feast** of these remarkable outfits.

<small>James Boekbinder</small>

Models emerge left and exit right, showing designs by Saskia van Drimmelen.

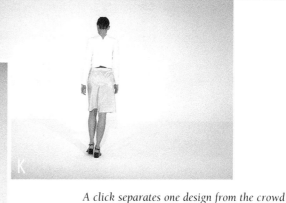

A click separates one design from the crowd for examination.

Another design by Saskia van Drimmelen on display. The small icon on the left shows us an animation of the pattern.

Pinch / Brad Johnson

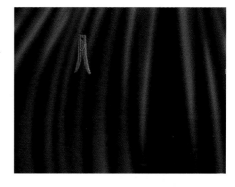

Disguised as a product demonstration for a fictitious **clothespin** company, Pinch is a lively, self–promotional diskette mailer that showcases the multimedia services of its designer Brad Johnson. Only five minutes in length and entirely self–running —that is, there are no opportunities for interaction — the promotion seamlessly integrates animation, sound, text and illustration, and as a result, reveals both the skills of its designer and the potential of digital multimedia as an effective graphic communication tool.

The promotion comprises a series of looped, animated segments that chart the advantages of 'Pinch Brand' clothespins. Ranging from upbeat and theatrical to cool and exacting in tone, these segments include an introductory title sequence and overview, a breakdown of the clothespin's design features, a sequence about the **woods** from which the clothespins are made and a summarising conclusion.

Pinch's opening sequence sets the stage for the light–hearted theatrics that will ensue: first, the words Brad Johnson Presents fade in, followed by a red–curtained stage to which a clothespin enters and stands under a spotlight. The text then fades out, and the clothespin quickly pirouettes to the left and upwards off the screen.

145

As Pinch's title sequence unfolds, the company logo and motto are introduced, as is a brief overview of the entire promotion.

Year of publication 1995 **Author** Brad Johnson **Place of publication** Berkeley, CA, USA **Publisher** Brad Johnson **Copyright owner** Brad Johnson **Awards** Communication Arts Interactive Design Annual '95: Winner, ID Magazine Annual Design Review '95: Honorable Mention, HOW Magazine Self-Promotional Annual '95: Outstanding Achievement, New Media Magazine Invision Awards '95: Finalist **Design company** Brad Johnson presents **Screen design** Brad Johnson **Animation / graphics** Brad Johnson **Sound design** Jeff Stafford **Contributors** Jeff Stafford, Bonnie Smetts **Software used** AI, APS, SSP, AS, MMD, MMS, QXP **Platform** mac

Pinch's visual style, like its subject matter, is decidedly **low-tech.** A nostalgia for a pre–digital era pervades the presentation's design, whether it be the choice of typography, illustration or musical score. Each screen is fairly minimal in composition, so that when a word or image is introduced, it retains its identity as an individual element. The sequences of screens are also pared down, avoiding the tendency most promotions have to overload their audience with excessive information.

Pinch does not sacrifice visual flare for the sake of clarity. Although the overall pacing is somewhat slow, text and images are introduced at a steady enough rate to maintain the viewer's interest. Probably most significant to the promotion's overall graphic character is the use of **fade-ins** as a transitional device. A new sequence is defined as the whole screen fades to black, and similarly, within sequences, text and images punctuate each other as they alternately appear from and dissolve into mere pixels. This technique builds and releases anticipation, as it also focuses the viewer's attention on the information being presented.

In what could be called a morphing sequence, the block of green manzanita wood transforms into a clothespin of the same material.

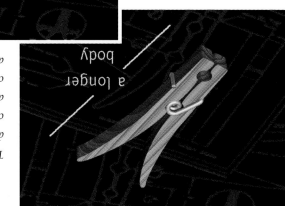

FROM THE
MENDOCINO
COAST...

CALIFORNIA

Green Manzanita

double-gauge
brass alloy
spring

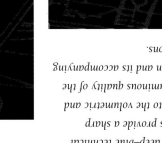

consistent
in-line tracking

The flat, deep–blue technical drawings provide a sharp contrast to the volumetric and almost luminous quality of the clothespin and its accompanying annotations.

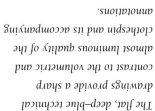

a longer
body

The promotion is enlivened by additional animation techniques, such as varying the way text unfolds and moving objects within the screen in both two and three dimensions. Typography and colour are also manipulated to modulate emphasis, as the screens frequently rotate the use of a classic cursive script and a bold, block–lettered type, and alternate between a bright and more subdued palette.

On the whole, Pinch's lack of interactive opportunity is negligible to the **self-promotion** format. In fact, as a light–hearted blend of the fantastic and real, it is a welcome alternative to the more sober, interactive, slideshow–formatted, digital portfolios.

MELISSA DALLAL

The first appearance of an entirely black and white screen heightens the impact of the vibrant and elaborately rendered screen that follows.

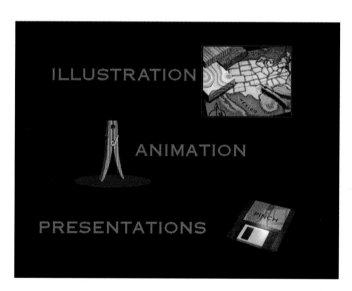

As Pinch winds down, the three–part introductory menu is recapitulated in a second three–part menu that features the designer's services.

V.O.L.V.O. Airbag / Paul Groot, Jans Possel

V.O.L.V.O. *Airbag* features the Dutch pop group V.O.L.V.O. (an acronym that roughly translates as 'Association Under Its Own Auspices'), featuring new music (the band's single number Airbag in a series of re–mixes by DJs) and performances by the three–member group, as well as a wealth of other experiences, including friends, **enemies,** poetry, text, photography and movies.

Introducing Lennart, the 'theatre' in V.O.L.V.O. (from introductory sequence).

Classic film projection motifs accompany one throughout the showings. Users type in their name in the beginning; it then accompanies them as they move through the disc (note user names in red letters between movie screen and cursor).

A swimmer briefly taps at our window to get our attention.

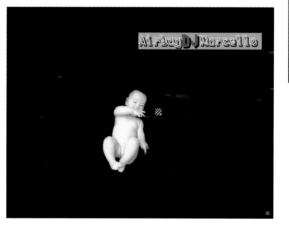

Boogying babies, alone and in pairs, often drift by as we listen to the re–mixes. Only real babies can dance that happily (even thought the directors have lent them a choreographic hand here to help keep in step). Note the cursor, which renews its shape with each new section.

Year of publication 1995 **Author** Paul Groot, Jans Possel **Place of publication** Amsterdam, Netherlands **Publisher** Paul Groot, Jans Possel **Copyright owners** Paul Groot, Jans Possel **Awards** Apple, MTV Advertisement **Screen design** Paul Groot, Jans Possel **Animation / graphics** Sander Hassing, Mari Soppola, Martin Loquet, Joost Meerman, Igor Teeuwen **Interaction design** Paul Groot, Jans Possel, Yariv Alter Fin **Sound design** Richard Cameron and Deejays **Production** Paul Groot, Jans Possel, V.O.L.V.O. **Editors** Paul Groot, Jans Possel **Contributors** V.O.L.V.O., Pochi, AH, Chris Remie, Francina Monkau, Guido Schrijvers, and many others **Platform** mac

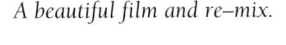

Airbag Kaap
/Anemaet

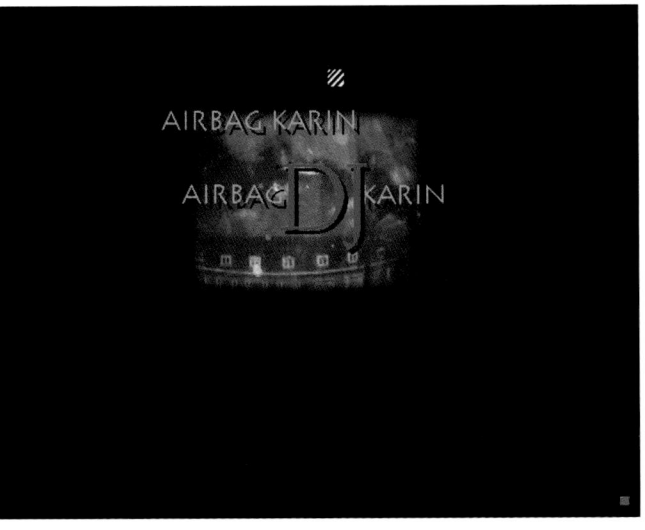

Pochi, the 'airfield–signalling' operator, is a recurring figure in the disc. Here, he is partially obscured by the icon to which he is calling to our attention.

A beautiful film and re–mix.

150

Viewers find themselves in a vast, dark movie projection space (a nice touch is that this extends to the edges of larger screens, extending the dark theatre beyond the viewing window). The beautifully innovative Angel–coded interface causes movies and accompanying elements **to float** in the darkness, jostling, obscuring and revealing each other in response to the movement of the cursor. This visual design turns the tables on what have consistently been called the shortcomings and 'loss of quality' of moving images in CD–ROMs: the choppiness of movement, small size, low resolution and colour limitations. Here, plunged into darkness, all of those same qualities combine to make these miniature movies visual gems bursting with atmosphere.

The main interface. Leaving the cursor on the Enemies of V.O.L.V.O panel has brought a massive, powerful symbolic opponent to life. Give him a tap (if you dare) to find other rivals of V.O.L.V.O.

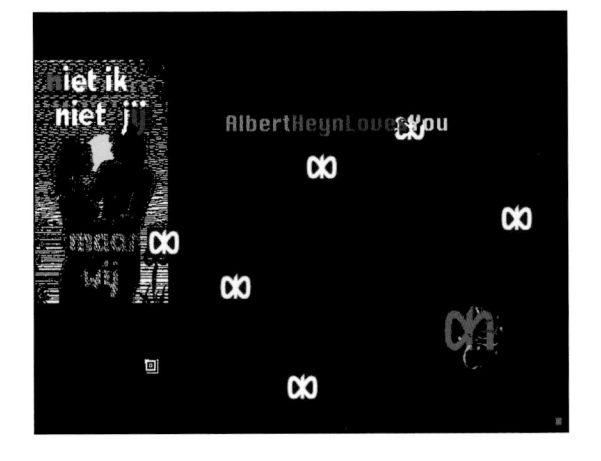

Artist Arnoud Holleman's supermarket world holds everything in life. Here, a swarm of angel–coded, graphic butterflies flutters in the darkness surrounding an embracing couple. Expressive texts complete the effect.

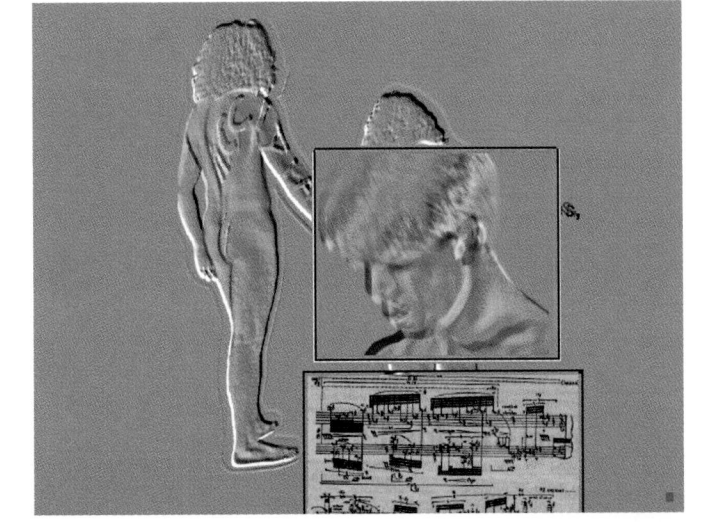

Composition with mathematical formula, musical score, text and people.

After the introduction, in which we meet V.O.L.V.O. members Pinky, Richard and Lennart, we arrive at the main interface: a panel punctuated by rectangles in relief. Simply moving the cursor to the right or left of field causes it to scroll; if the cursor is left on one of the links for a moment, the rectangular relief comes to life and gives a **preview** of what it conceals.

Various artists, performances and works of art can be evoked and explored here. What this disc achieves is a great deal more than simply selecting and 'showcasing' works. It comes as close as anything can to allowing viewers to feel what artistic composition is like. What really links the enormously varied parts of the disc are art's most basic impulses and strategies of inclusion, combination, displacement and rejection. In Salman Rushdie's Satanic Verses as Inspiration for a Blue Movie, a live 'talking head' (Rushdie) explains his book and the controversy surrounding it, while surrounding written texts shed light on the implications of other media forms for the composition of text in our time and the Satanic Verses in particular (of special importance in this connection is the animated film **cartoon** and its scenario; we can view two live cartoons in accompaniment to the written texts). Anonymous Friends uses similar strategies to create a biting portrait of human enthusiasm.

Once adrift in this disc, viewers find themselves in a darkness pervaded by a special atmosphere in which things seen are not easily forgotten.

JAMES BOEKBINDER

Otto draws. Occasionally, his own creations drift in to have a look at what he's doing.

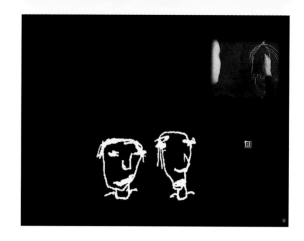

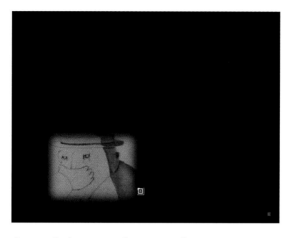

Startled awakening: the beginning of an animated film catches its hero napping.

151

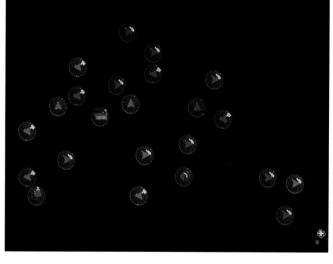

Floating bubbles contain samples of the re-mixes. Viewers can select and re-combine them as they see fit.

From the Blue Movie. Salman Rushdie talks about The Satanic Verses while the text (and movie) helps us to understand the influence of animated cartoons.

Location: http://www.xs4all.nl/~sculptro/index.htm

About this shopping mall.

Related links.

Enter.

Mail me.

Home of Lars.

Offer me a job.

On arrival at the Shopping Mall, the customer encounters the dumbbell clickable map. The left ball opens when clicked, giving a choice of three destinations: the fashion shop, the beauty farm or the tattoo shop.

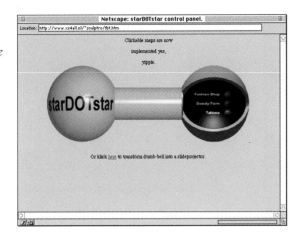

The importance of personal and corporate representation on the World Wide Web is rapidly developing into a recognised necessity. Elaborate corporate web sites are becoming an integral part of the public relations and communication industry. But how do you present yourself on a private or **personal** level? What image do you create on your homepage?

Incorporating this very question, Amsterdam–based artist Sculptro (digital alter–ego for Lars Eijssen) created a web site that is at once personal and professional. Elaborating on the design and structure of on–line shopping facilities, he developed the StarDOTstar Shopping Mall. This Mall 'houses' some small boutiques that specialise in **modifying** the virtual body. In the fashion shop, the tattoo shop or the beauty farm, customers can have their digital image dressed in one of Sculptro's creations, their virtual body embellished, enhanced, mutilated or transplanted. Surf the web in your own, private, real, Eijssen space sock!

The dumbbell can also be turned into a slide projector. Don't forget to turn off the light.

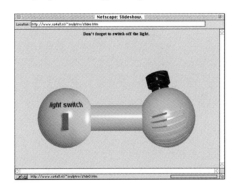

Two slides show examples of Sculptro's work. Clicking on the green text presents the next slide.

153

Year of publication 1995 Author Lars Eijssen Place of publication http://www.xs4all.nl/~sculptro/index.htm

Publisher Lars Eijssen Copyright owner Lars Eijssen Design company Lars Eijssen Screen design Lars Eijssen Animation / graphics Lars Eijssen

Interaction design Lars Eijssen Sound design Lars Eijssen Production Lars Eijssen Editor Lars Eijssen Platform www

What to wear on your home page? Shop for the latest custom-made Netwear at House of Sculptro.

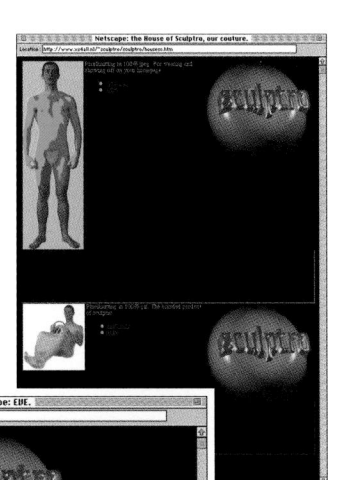

The House of Sculptro presents its latest creations, 'Eve' and the 'Spacesock'. More information and an order form are only a mouse click away.

The opening page presents the menu in form of a dumbbell, the principal icon of the body–enhancement craze in the physical world. Clicking the dumbbell allows you to enter the individual shops. However, it also **transforms** into a slide projector. After you have switched off the light, you can help yourself to an actual slide show of Sculptro's work. Light emanates from the projector and a bright green DOS–prompt indicates the spot to click for the next slide.

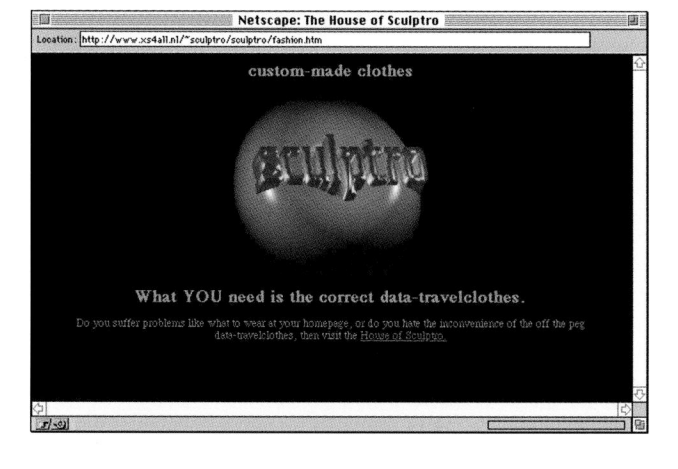

The clickable map of the dumbbell takes you to the House of Sculptro, the on–line **fashion store.** It offers a choice of custom–made data–travel clothes. Two pixelknitted creations, 'Eve' and 'Spacesock', modelled here by Sculptro himself, can be obtained by way of a regular order form. It invites you to send a scanned image of yourself, which will be returned to you dressed in new attire and ready for use on your homepage.

154

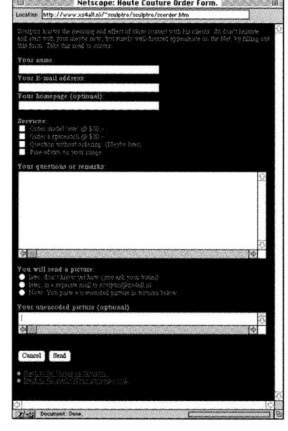

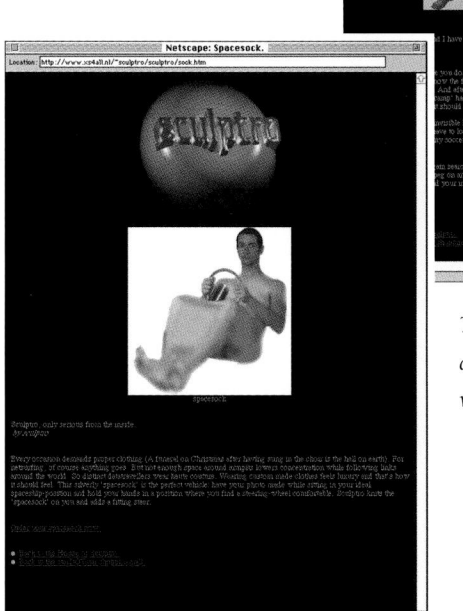

These fully pixelknitted creations were designed for sale on the Net. Web-surfing will never be the same again.

How to order your very own bodysock? Just fill out the form and mail a digital image of yourself to the House of Sculptro. For a modest fee, Sculptro will return it, dressed to thrill.

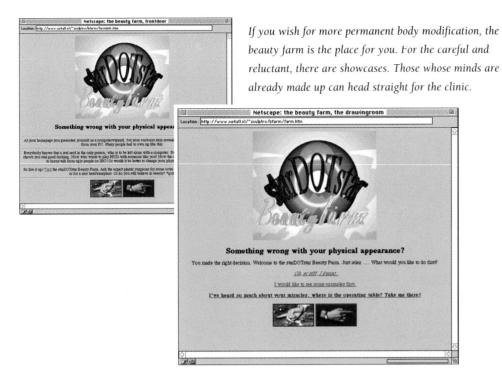

If you wish for more permanent body modification, the beauty farm is the place for you. For the careful and reluctant, there are showcases. Those whose minds are already made up can head straight for the clinic.

For the full body treatment, you simply give detailed instructions. Doctor and nurse will take good care of you.

The beauty farm offers a further range of modification facilities and a collection of showcases, for those who feel there is something **wrong** with their physical appearance. For the moment, the tattoo shop is only represented by a continuously reloaded commercial, apologising but promising new possibilities.

StarDOTstar is a well–designed site, combining personal and professional information. It uses the possibilities of multiple reloading, transforming objects or simply changing backgrounds in a very **clever** way, and really engages the visitor to explore and ultimately purchase his new, virtual persona.

GEERT J. STRENGHOLT

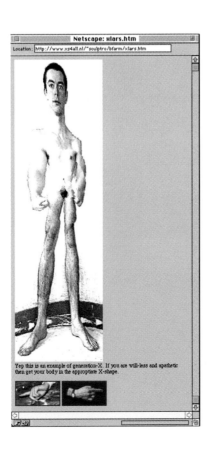

The tattoo shop is closed, for the moment. A continuously reloaded commercial entices viewers to return at some future date.

To demonstrate their treatments, the beauty farm features several examples. Clicking the lower icons allows you to explore other examples.

ZeitMovie & Selected Notes 2 ZeitGuys
Bob Aufuldish

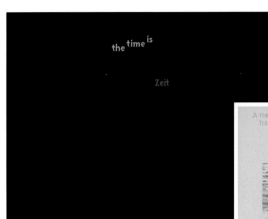

Two shots taken from the opening sequence of the Zeitmovie. A collage of image and text exploring concepts of time and language.

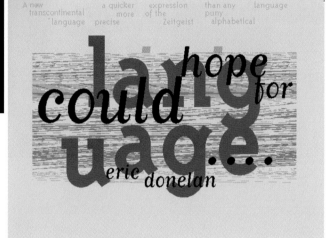

157

In a way, both Selected Notes 2 ZeitGuys and ZeitMovie are semi–interactive **portfolios** on floppy disc of ZeitGuys, an illustrated font developed by Emigré. Both productions attempt to connect and give meaning to a collection of one hundred and twenty–six illustrations in font format.

Allowing hardly any interactive meddling, the ZeitMovie simply presents a collage of ZeitGuys–images flashing across the screen in bright colours. Clicking an appearing and disappearing icon takes you to a second–level presentation, showing complete pages. In a second window, a close–up sweeps across the page producing another fragmented collage effect.

This main screen of the ZeitMovie presents a continuous stream of bright red images on center screen. Clicking the small green shape in the left–hand corner gives access to the second level of the presentation.

Year of publication 1995 **Author** Bob Aufuldish **Place of publication** CA, USA **Publisher** Emigre, Zed the journal of the Center for Design Studies at Virginia Commonwealth University

Copyright owners Aufuldish & Warinner **Awards** ZeitMovie: I.D. Annual Design Review '95, Type Directors Club, Typography 16; Selected Notes 2 ZeitGuys: Interactive Design 1 '95, sponsored by CA magazine

Design company Aufuldish & Warinner **Screen design** Bob Aufuldish **Animation / graphics** Eric Donelan, Bob Aufuldish **Interaction design** Bob Aufuldish

Sound design Bob Aufuldish, Scott Pickering (ZeitMovie) **Production** Bob Aufuldish **Editors** Mark Bartlett **Contributors** David Karam (scripting Selected Notes 2 ZeitGuys) **Software used** MMD, MMS **Platform** mac

ZeitGuys designers Eric Donelan and Bob Aufuldish, the latter of design firm Aufuldish & Warinner, meant to create images purposefully **lacking** intended meaning – images that would acquire meaning rather than be pre-determined. They started experimenting with contextualising these images, allowing them to form a new poetic language. For Selected Notes they asked Mark Bartlett to compose a text among their world of images, thus redefining the image–language. Bartlett's text is based on French cultural theory and deconstruc-tionist practice, and tries to bridge image and text, graphic design and writing. The result is a mixture of text, image and sound that resembles most closely the surrealist exquisite corpse.

Title page of the Selected Notes. The page slowly fades into a blurred, unreadable image.

Sel ected NOTES a ZeitGuys

Selected Notes to ZeitGuys

Bob Aufuldish
statement about the design

Mark Bartlett
statement about the text

Eric Donelan
statement about the images

Before entering the Selected Notes, the table of contents gives extra information. Clicking on the menu dots will release texts by the authors.

**non sense
sense non
non sense
sense**

see again | notes to ZeitGuys | exit

The final menu allows you to play the movie again, look at notes or exit the program through a sequence of credits.

What it tracks there is the trace of imminent return. a gesturalness, speechless agitation that channels the suppressed into a precipitous onrushing through associations of metonomic, It tracks in the absence of the fragments, (which are always already defered), and before the presence of the signers to the contract. What it allocates are moments of symbolic ruration of contract, that restores the possibility of recognizing the historic continuity of an original spoken moment, of affirmation. It is this affirmation this immediacy formed in the presence of the signers that Derrida excludes from the domain of human activity. Experience is that which cannot be written and therefore, paradoxically, not experienced.

n the domain of human
that which cannot be
doxically, not experienced.

notes

Underneath the continuous movie runs a presentation of individual pages. The window on the right shows the entire page, while the smaller window on the left shows a continuous moving close-up of the page. The two clenched fists are used to move to the next or previous page.

PUN Punching
"Rol and the Bar Man is de ad

In essence, the basic interface consists of paging back and forth through blurry black–and–white pages that only reveal their contents when the mouse is run across them. Snippets of text and images pop up as you roll over them, sometimes accompanied by sound. Aufuldish calls it **navigating** the page. This random appearance contrasts sharply with the seemingly linear order of page's. However, it invites you to play around, construct new connections and new readings, revealing the pages' implicit or covert meaning. The cursor seems to tease some sense out of different, overlapping layers of meaning.

The designs and images are quirky and fresh, the texts sometimes obscure, sometimes ironic. In view of the fact that both ZeitMovie and Selected Notes 2 ZeitGuys were created for a floppy disc format, the designs are remarkably elaborate.

GEERT J. STRENGHOLT

ZeitGuys is a collection of 126 images in font format which form a new poetical language to buttress the burned-out shell which is alphabetic communication.

ZeitGuys is an endless "Exquisite Corpse" with each author redefining the image-language, infusing it with particular meaning where before there was none.

Moreover, because of the prevalence of font piracy worldwide, these images will become global, and have the potential to become symbols with different meanings in different cultures. Thus ZeitGuys could be thought of as the first symbol virus to spread worldwide.

In this introduction, Eric Donelan explains what ZeitGuys is about.

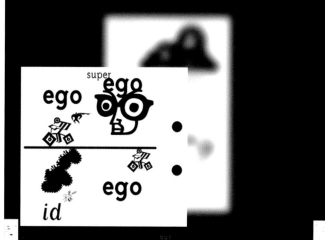

159

Various examples of pages in the Selected Notes showing pop–up texts and images. In the background, the blurred pages from which these fragments came are still visible. The two small pages in the left– and right–hand corner are used to 'leaf' through the material.

Reference

The Library: Authors L–Z (click and hold to view title)

BEN SHNEIDERMAN
Designing the User Interface: Strategies for Effective Human-Computer Interaction, 1992

DOORS OF PERCEPTION 1, MEDIAMATIC INTERACTIVE
PUBLISHING, 1994

'Looking up' something is an activity that demands a lot more hand–work than the expression suggests. The design of libraries and reference sources is therefore traditionally devoted to shortening the distance between hand and eye as much as possible. The hand is directed to the right shelf in the bookcase and from there to the right volume, the right page, the right lemma. Dictionaries and encyclopaedia make use of a highly specialised set of typographical conventions and signs, all concerned with linear ordering of information. This way of accessing information in print works very smoothly (with sufficient shelf space). But as soon as cross–referencing enters the picture, books become a tiresome medium. A case in point is the Treasury, a magnificent combination of dictionary, list of synonyms and etymological explanations — and one that often produces sore fingers. This kind of cross–referential source has been

waiting for centuries for multimedia to solve its usability problem! While the book format may not survive the great leap forward in this field, the book metaphor probably will. Once the sought–for information has reached the screen, the standard conventions of page layout and typography prove to be very strong and functional indeed. But are they fit for the job?

Hands–on accessibility of information is almost everything when it comes to reference sources. The interesting thing about reference works in interactive multimedia is that the designer can endow the structure of this 'random' access with a narrative logic of its own. Besides road–signing the highway to the entries, there is an opportunity to point to different kinds of detours, linking the information in a way that suggests the structure of a body of knowledge instead of a collection of single items. The designer has to provide compasses for those who leave the highway.

This kind of interactivity not only requires the clear typography of the 'Question & Answer' approach. It can also mean visually enabling the browser to sort out the intertext between the answers. This calls for different graphic codes and metaphors, most of which have yet to be fully developed. 'Looking up' becomes 'looking around' in a three–dimensional maze of hyperlinked information sources. Screen design here is not only concerned with ordering the answers, but must assist the user in moving around in this vast space and taking what they need from it. It calls for a combination of the graphic codes of library, transportation schedule, shopping mall and registration office with the conventions of architectural representation. Something new, that is.

MAX BRUINSMA

THE NEW WAY THINGS WORK

DAVID MACAULAY

The Way Things Work / David Macaulay

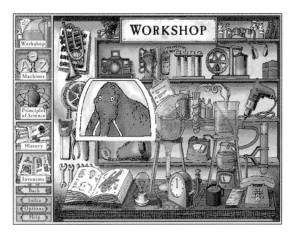

...the Workshop, with a voice–over introducing the (animated!) devices on the bench and the main interface on the left. Note the woolly mammoth assistant rolling out of the printer as it is introduced.

The Way Things Work, a guide to the world of technology by author and illustrator David Macaulay, can only be called a **mammoth** achievement. Remember the sheer delight of being suddenly released from regular lessons to pile into a dark room at school and watch cartoons? Macaulay has combined this with the qualities of an ideal pedagogical mentor who is never at a loss for an answer to the literally endless questions crowding the mind of any curious child or adult confronted with this material.

The Way Things Work illuminates the world of technology from its peaks of **engineering** down to its very roots in physics. The interface is a simple stack of five panels (Workshop, Machines A–Z, Principles of Science, History, Inventors) and three drawers full of Options, Credits and Help. Typography has been kept simple, with important terms and links highlighted in red. Different kinds of links are clearly distinguished.

...the 'S' section of the alphabetically organised, scrolled catalogue of machines.

Opening screen of The A–Z of Machines. A crowd gasps as a monolithic 'S' is stamped, followed by...

163

Year of publication 1994 **Author** David Macaulay **Place of publication** UK, USA, Canada, Australia **Publisher** Dorling Kindersley
Copyright owners David Macauly, Dorling Kindersley, Houghton Mifflin **Design company** Dorling Kindersley **Platform** mac / mpc

The submarine explained. Red highlights identify links, with clear typographic distinction of the basic underlying concepts of physics (glossary links in main text at left), main activities of the submarine and its most important component parts. Note mammoth assistant giving animated impression of submarine at top left. The See Also at bottom right offers links to scuba, ship and sailboat.

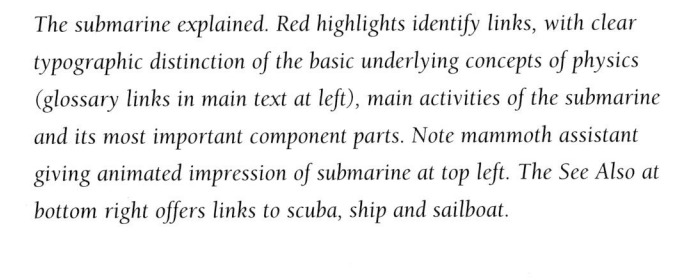

The Workshop is a picture of a bench and shelves cluttered with an assortment of solid, handmade–looking devices. It sets the down–to–earth, hands–on tone that pervades the graphic design of the entire disc. In the A–Z of Machines, we use a **gigantic** machine to gain access to a scrollable, alphabetised directory of machines. The Inventors' biographies are arranged in an illustrated scrapbook that can be paged through using red alphabet tabs, with links to inventions. The History time line stretches all the way back to 7000 BC. Principles of Science takes us to a kind of technology park, with demonstrations on platforms labelled with major concepts.

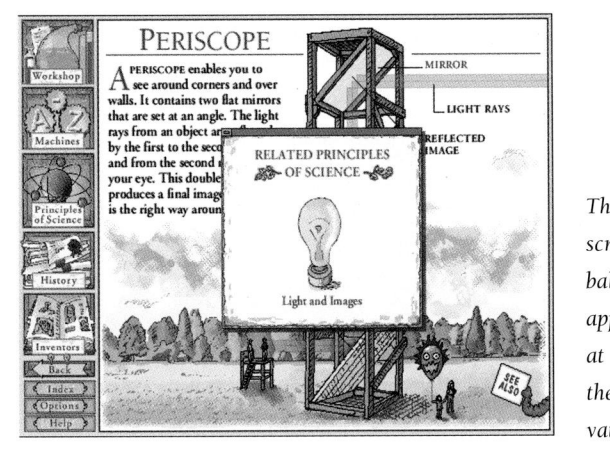

The periscope merits a new, full–screen explanation, with animated balloon about to ascend and appear to observers on platform at right (partially concealed by the Basic Principles window activated by the interface at left, devoted to Light and Image).

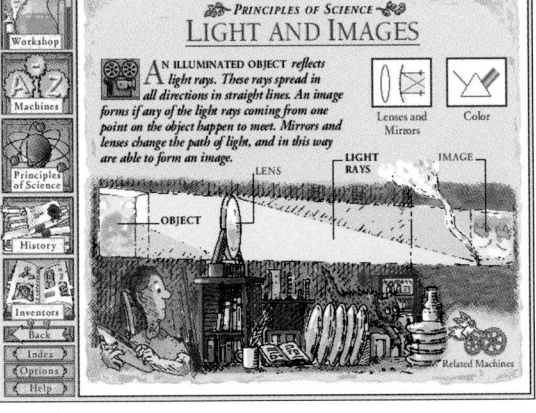

Hydroplane link: an animated submarine dives and surfaces, accompanied by full sound and written explanation.

Onward to a full–scale explanation of Light and Image, but not before we've hit the projector at top right to have the whole complex business tied together by...

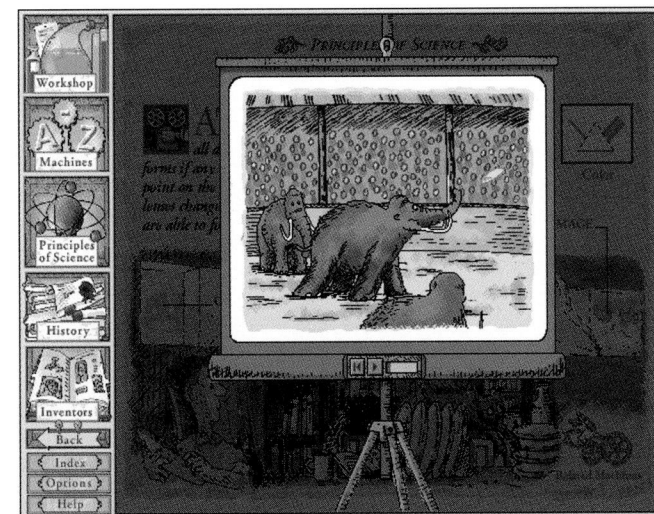

...a Mammoth Movie taking us to the Crystal Discus Event at the Mammoth Olympics (popular, but very problematic!). Lights down on Basic Principles in the background, for the moment.

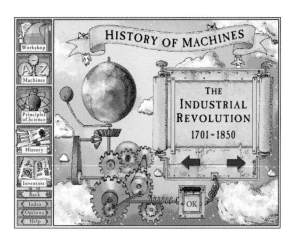

History of Machines. The main screen with scroll device offering major epochs.

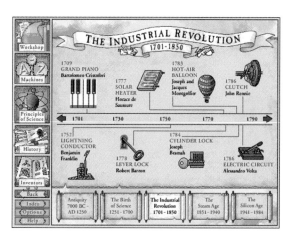

History of Machines time line with inventors and machines.

The disc is richly endowed with funny contraptions and concise animated diagrams using voice–overs and written explanations. The straightforward, clear design is offset by a whole herd of ingenious, expressive mammoths, who point the way, demonstrate technology, provide comic relief and — star in a series of Mammoth Movies (complete with the flickering and unholy racket of a real 16mm projector)! These minuscule, incredibly **funny movies** capture the viewer's heart and mind utterly, as well as virtually every single engineering milestone from 7000 BC to the present. When the lights go up, we find the screens from the Principles of Science section with the main concepts touched on by the damsel–in–distress–saving (Screw Thread), movie–stunting (Friction), lemon–picking (Electricity), discus–throwing (Light and Images) mammoths.

Besides its engaging style of illustration, The Way Things Work owes it effectiveness to its author's wonderful sense of humour: certainly the ultimate source of pedagogical links, with its refreshing disregard for any road–too–often–taken and its inherent love of unexpected connections.

JAMES BOEKBINDER

Inventors. The scrapbook open at 'A'.

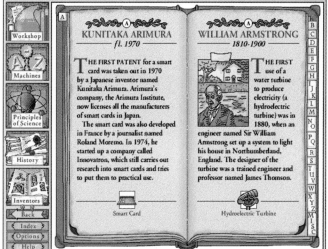

Further along in 'A': note links to machines at bottom of pages.

165

W. Armstrong's hydroelectric turbine explained. Active link to water wheel, complete with animated demonstration by woolly mammoth.

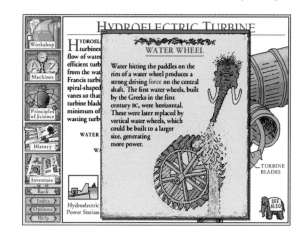

Mankind Before Man

Cryo Interactive Entertainment, Louis- Michel Désert

The evolutionary origin of mankind, with its immense time scale, branching structure and parallel stories, is an ideal topic to take full advantage of the CD medium's strengths. Edited by Yves Coppens, **palaeontology** professor at the Collège de France, Mankind Before Man not only looks and feels good to use, it also almost pulls it off in the content department.

From the rat–like Purgatorius of seventy million years ago to Cro–Magnon man, via all major species, Mankind Before Man tells the story in a number of different and complimentary ways. Simple yet **scientific** throughout, crammed with Latin terms and dates, the opening interface uses the familiar desktop metaphor, with clickable objects accessing nine sections. The overall design of Mankind Before Man made use of the most recent programming technologies: full motion video sequences, 3D–rendered animations accompanied by genuine sounds, vocals, music and amazing morphing sequences.

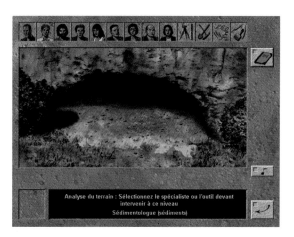

The beginning of an archaeological dig involves choosing a specialist from the team of nine or a tool from four. Voice–overs give feedback, during which the user learns about when and where pollen specialists, palaeontologists and bone experts are used, why, and how they interact with others to build a rich and detailed picture of a site.

167

The customised morphs are one of the most interactive elements of Mankind Before Man. Here, clicking on the red pointer then indicating which of man's ancestors to begin a morph from, and on the green pointer followed by an end species, combined with choosing whether to see body/skeleton/head or skull morph, and angle of view, results in a huge number of possible mini–movies.

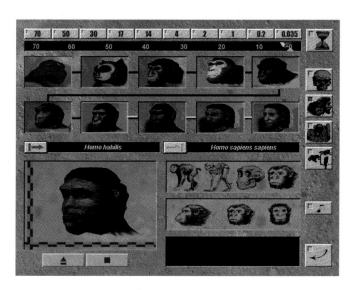

Year of publication 1995 **Author** Cryo Interactive Entertainment, Louis-Michel Désert **Place of publication** France **Publisher** Microfolie's Éditions **Copyright owners** Microfolie's Éditions, Cryo Interactive Entertainment **Awards** Prix Möbius '95, Prix Classe Multimédia '95 **Design company** Cryo Interactive Entertainment, Louis-Michel Désert **Screen design** Martial Brard **Animation / graphics** Rémy Benoit, Bernard Bittler, Martial Brard, Valérie Féruglio, Philippe Jédar, Frédéric Pinasseau **Interaction design** Emmanuel Nedelec **Sound design** Jean-Michel Toulon **Production** Cryo, Louis-Michel Désert **Editors** Microfolie's Éditions **Contributors** Louis-Michel Désert, Yves Coppens **Platform** mac/mpc/cdi

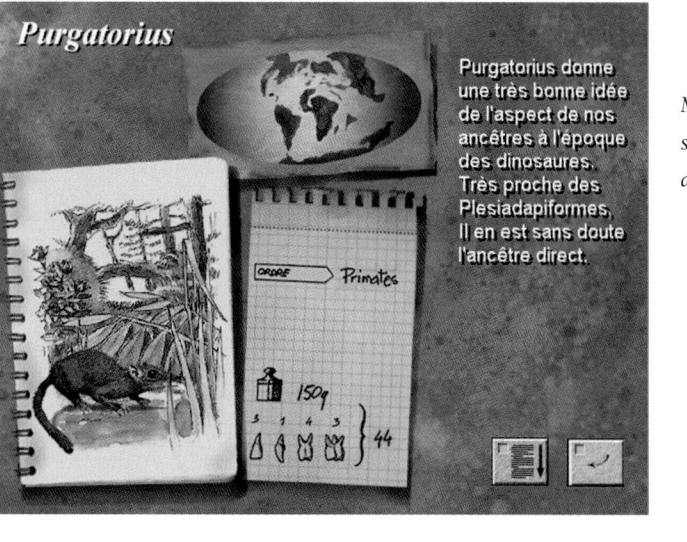

Purgatorius donne une très bonne idée de l'aspect de nos ancêtres à l'époque des dinosaures. Très proche des Plesiadapiformes, il en est sans doute l'ancêtre direct.

Much of the information in Mankind Before Man is presented via a notebook metaphor, mixing sketches, photos and archaeological artefacts with brief texts.

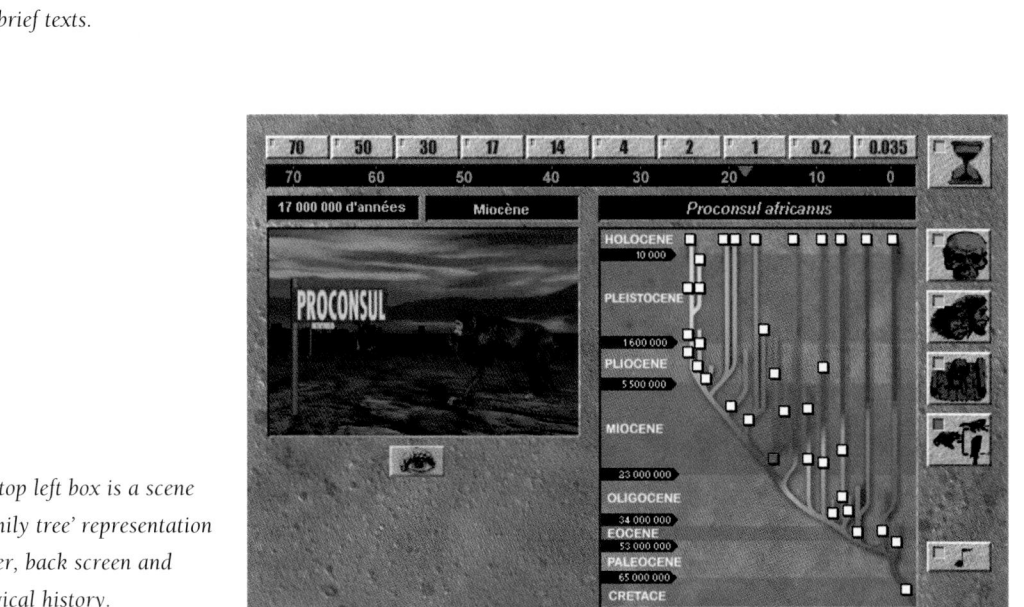

Cryo 3D's gaming techniques as applied to education. The top left box is a scene from a 3D virtual landscape visualising the traditional 'family tree' representation of man's ancestors. Icons (right) allow for change of chapter, back screen and sound level. The time line (top) locates the action in geological history.

The evolutionary origins of man are (perhaps too) firmly contextualised by brief passages on competing historical theories, from Ussher's Creationism of 1650, through Linné, Lamarck, Cuvier's Catastrophism and the Uniformitarianism of Lyell, and finally to **Darwin,** Mendel, molecular evolution and palaeontology.

The user can also go on a virtual archaeological expedition, where staff have to be picked and appropriate instruments chosen in a 'Question & Answer' session that's surprisingly trying and offers interesting **insights** into the process of discovery and the specialisation of modern–day digs.

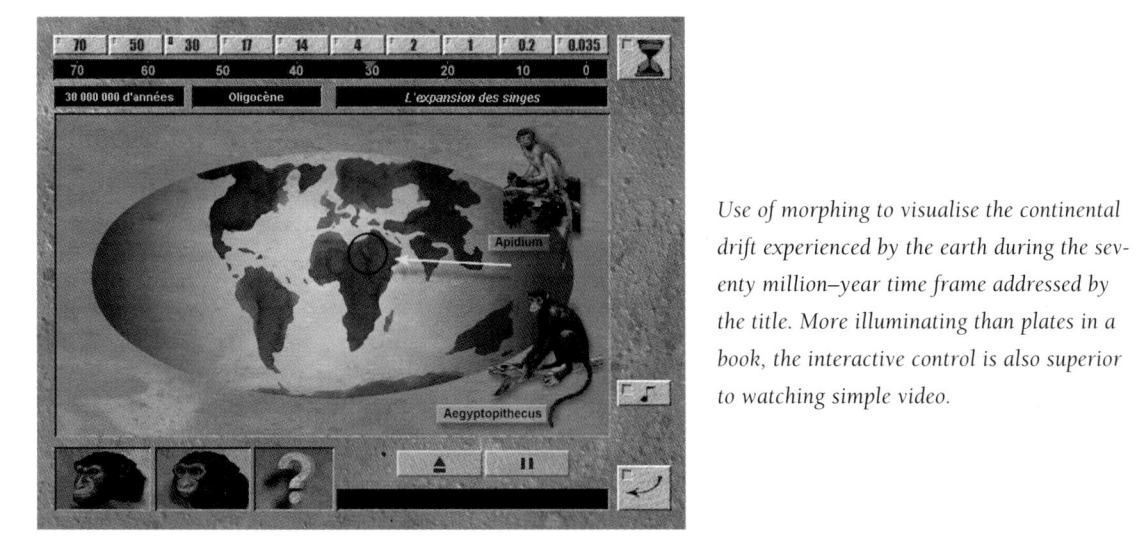

Use of morphing to visualise the continental drift experienced by the earth during the seventy million–year time frame addressed by the title. More illuminating than plates in a book, the interactive control is also superior to watching simple video.

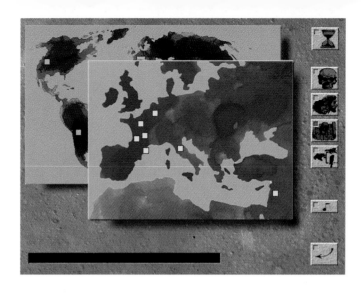

Nested maps in the Archaeological Discoveries chapter allow rapid access to voice–annotated slide shows of major dig sites.

Palaeontological Discoveries are illustrated with an excellent series of rotatable 3D models of head, skull and skeleton, animated maps that change to show the **tectonic** movement of the continents, giving a terrific sense of biological and geological change. Each continent has clickable points representing major finds. Clever use of voice–over, diaries, photos and objects builds a human–faced picture of the enterprise.

If any disc can answer the question: what does this add to books or videos?, this can. Games maker Cryo–3D's gaming skills have been admirably extended to their first 'edutainment' title. Graphic representations of time and change on the disc work well, carefully avoiding the USA Today syndrome — fancy graphs and charts devoid of meaning. Intellectual as well as aesthetic judgement has been well–exercised.

There is also a witty Evolutionary **family album** mock up and a 3D virtual landscape representing evolutionary time, through which the user cruises, passing signs such as You are now leaving the Cretaceous. These seemingly throw–away gimmicks subconsciously add a nice sense of comparative scale to both time and size difference.

JULES MARSHALL

169

Dry subject matter need not necessarily lead to dry presentation, and humour can be a motivator. Here, in test mode, the familiar icons representing human ancestors are used to assign a level to the student's score. Being rated an 'Australopithecine' was a greater incentive to try again than '6/10'.

Brief introductory essays on the competing theories of human origins set the stage for the discussion of modern ideas and discoveries. The 'book' visual metaphor combines with the 'notebooks' of other chapters to give Mankind a pleasant 'academic–study–on–a–disc' feel.

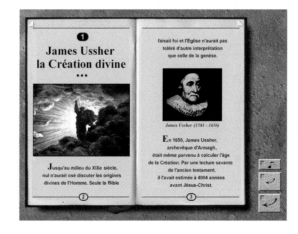

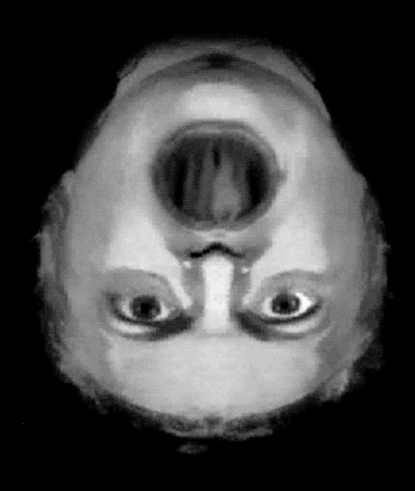

Enough!

change • volume

Doors of Perception 1
Mediamatic Interactive Publishing

Doors of Perception 1 (DoPRom), made by
the Dutch publisher Mediamatic
Interactive Publishing for the Netherlands
Design Institute, employs a subtle, distinctive visual language. DoPRom's
objective was to present the most
attractive and valuable aspects of the
Doors of Perception conference organised
by the Netherlands Design Institute and
Mediamatic in October 1994. The first in a
series of mould–breaking conferences,
Doors of Perception covered a multitude
of issues concerned with the development
of **digital media** within
contemporary society. The disc is a record
of the interchange of attitudes and ideas
that took place during the two–day event.

After a brief introductory sequence, you enter the
conference's 'home space'. This is pervaded by a conference foyer
atmosphere, filled with **chatter** and ambient sound as
you scroll past twenty–one speakers, eight globes representing
different discussion themes and nine icons housing miscellaneous
additional information.

*The home space scrolls sensitively and at varying speeds,
depending on the positioning of your cursor. The sound is
also carefully orchestrated, subtly varying in quality as
you browse through the environment.*

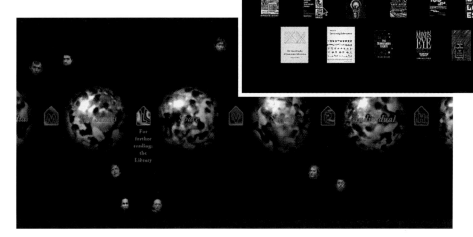

*Rolling your cursor over a house
icon reveals a caption indicating
additional content, such as a
library of related reading.*

171

*The help function is very comprehensive. It pro-
vides an overview of the home space together
with eleven screens of further information.*

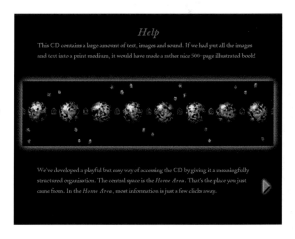

Year of publication 1994 **Author** Mediamatic Interactive Publishing **Place of publication** Amsterdam, Netherlands **Publisher** Netherlands Design Institute **Copyright owners** Mediamatic, Speakers of Doors 1

Awards New Voices New Visions '95: One of three Winners, Interactive Media Festival '95: Meta Design Award, I.D., Annual Design Review '95: Design Exellence Award, Amsterdam Art Council: Encouragement Prize Graphic Design '95,

Screen Multimedia Magazine: CD der Monat Januar '95 **Design company** Mediamatic Interactive Publishing **Screen design** Willem Velthoven **Animation / graphics** Willem Velthoven

Interaction design Willem Velthoven, Mari Soppela, Sander Hassing **Sound design** Leo Anemaet **Production** Kristi van Riet **Editors** Jules Marshall, Arie Altena **Software used** MMD, MMS, APS, APR, MMS **Platform** mac

Portraits of the speakers are suspended like miniature planets
of enlightenment in the darkness. As your cursor rolls over each
individual, a key word buzzes into the aural foreground. Select a
speaker, and you are presented with sampled texts from their
speeches and extracts of video footage from their presentations.
Subtle sub—menus comprise concise descriptions of the
various sections and allow access to speaker documentation and
relevant threads of discussion. To offset the potential austerity of
the speaker—and—text combination, a row of mouths at the bottom
of the screen provide entertaining, musical portraits with cut—up
words and sound extracts.

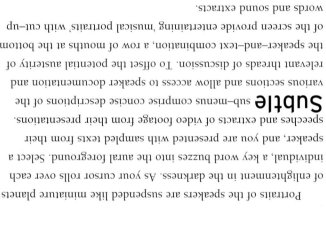

HEIM

The written is an ideational fix; we begin to use the
hand and the eye primarily to learn, to use the page.
The book becomes increasingly contemplative,
private. We separate ourselves off — we have our own
mindspace; we become individualistic.

*The opinion slider allows you to compose unique juxtapo-
sitions of quotes, depending on your own views.*

STEIN

Conceptually, why bother to go from books to something electronic?
The **breakthrough** in thinking for us was when we realised that...
stopped thinking about a book 'cause of it's physical nature, stopped
thinking about it in terms of the fact that it was ink on paper, 'n started
thinking about it in terms of the way it was used.
We realised that the book was the one technology, the one medium
where the user had complete control over the sequence and the pace in
which they access the material. And that it's a user-driven medium, as
opposed to let's say films or television or radio, which was a producer-
driven medium; somebody makes something 'n you sit there 'n you
experience it.
Well, we realised that by putting a book onto a dynamic medium, onto
a computer, that you could in fact have the same control over motion
pictures and audio that you have over text. So that if you thought of a
book 'cause of the way it's used, then you could start to include more
than just text. You could use audio and video in the same way so that a
book could include those things

STEIN: Physical books offer the user complete control. Putting books on computer
allows the same control over producer-driven media like film, radio and TV.

*The speakers' portraits yield an
in—depth view of each
individual's key ideas and
works. As the cursor rolls over a
mouth, extracts of texts lead you
onto other related threads of discussion.*

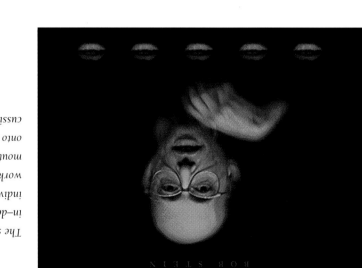

ROB STEIN

Portrait of Japanese media artist and conference participant Toshio Iwai.

Part of Toshio Iwai's lecture.

The sheer volume and complexity of the material presented by the speakers demands an imaginative and flexible interactive design. For this, Mediamatic tested and developed a unique interactive mechanism: an opinion slider which appears at the base of the screen. A **morphing face** grimaces at you in a range of contortions that represent subtle shifts in opinion from positive to negative. Thus, at any moment, you can cross–link from one speaker's comment to another based on your own predilection.

The visual style of the disc is clear and concise throughout, with no superfluous elements. Nothing distracts from the **synergy** of content and interactive structure. This disc is not just a vibrant record of a conference, but an attempt to explore the possibilities of a new and rapidly evolving medium.

GILES ROLLESTONE

173

Jeet Singh on Designing Electronic the Community.

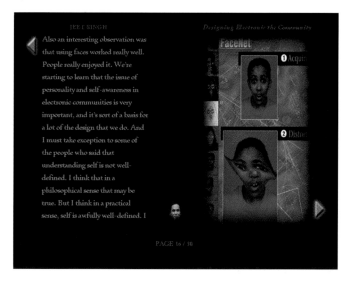

Lecturer Masuyama on the book/CD–ROM project Multimedia Frontier '93.

Le Louvre

Le Louvre

Le Louvre

peintures & palais

Le Louvre : Palace and Paintings

Dominique Brisson, Natalie Coural

Main interface. Note the guided tour at lower right and links to four sections of palace next to the main link with photograph of pyramid.

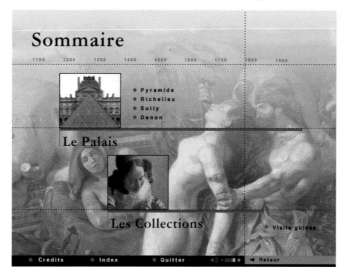

Anyone who has been to the Louvre museum in Paris knows how quickly and thoroughly the fatigue particular to museums takes hold of one's eyes, mind and feet while exploring it. The makers of Le Louvre: Peintures et Palais seem to have realised that even in virtual form, the sheer richness and volume of the Louvre and its collection can be exhausting for viewers. They have solved this potential problem brilliantly by being extremely **selective** and restrained, both in the structure of content and visual design. All voice and written information is very brief in duration, allowing one a lot of time to study the work and learn about it in silence, enlivened by occasional period music as one moves back or forwards through time.

Full–screen reproduction of one of the ten works in the guided tour: Rembrandt's Bathsheba.

175

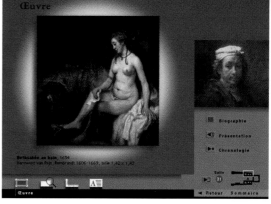

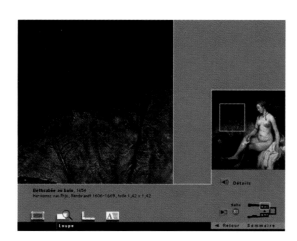

The magnifier in action.

Interface corresponding to the painting. Note the magnifying glass, measuring tool and A Propos icons at lower left, as well as commentary, biography, chronology and architectural links under artist's portrait.

Year of publication 1994 Author Dominique Brisson, Natalie Coural Place of publication Paris, France Publisher Montparnasse Multimédia, Réunion des Musées Nationaux

Copyright owners Montparnasse Multimédia, Réunion des Musées Nationaux Awards Milia d'Or '95 Screen design Montparnasse Multimédia, R.M.N., Index Animation / graphics Montparnasse Multimédia, R.M.N., Index

Interaction design Montparnasse Multimédia, R.M.N., Index Sound design Montparnasse Multimédia, R.M.N., Index Production Montparnasse Multimédia, R.M.N. Editors Montparnasse Multimédia, R.M.N. Contributors Index+ Platform mac

The painting in the background of the title sequence remains the background of the main interface (Sommaire). It is divided into two main sections (Le Palais and Les Collections), with four links to the various sections of the building and a **guided tour** at lower right. The tour leads through ten major works of the latter category (beautiful, full–screen representations), each provided with an interface resembling a dark space with light concentrated on the work of art and everything else one needs within easy reach in the semi–darkness. One can examine the work in detail using a magnifying glass, find out its scale with a measuring stick or gain essential background information with an A Propos link. Biography of the artist, chronology, commentary or a look at the work's location in the museum are also available.

The section about the building itself is somewhat more light and upbeat, with a time line through which we can find scale models accompanied by period music with links to floor plans and photographs of those same places today. The four links in the main interface to major sections provide information about their and their namesakes' history, as well as views of the floor plan today and a representative work (provided in turn with the interface and options mentioned above). In addition, a comprehensive **index** sub–divides the material into works, exhibitions and biographies.

Using the measuring instrument to find out the painting's scale.

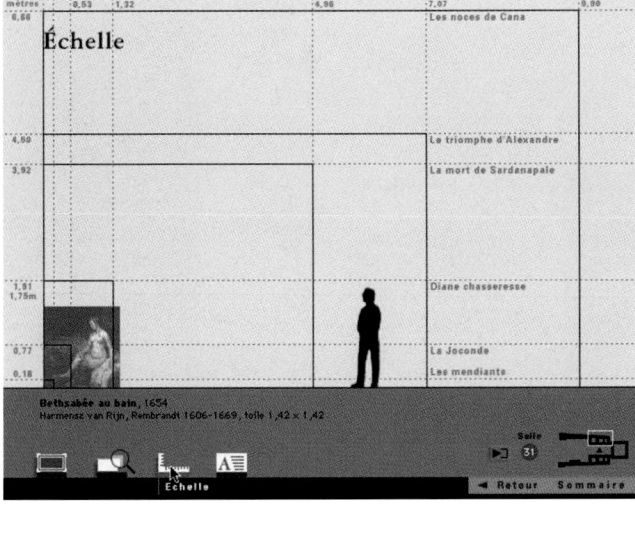

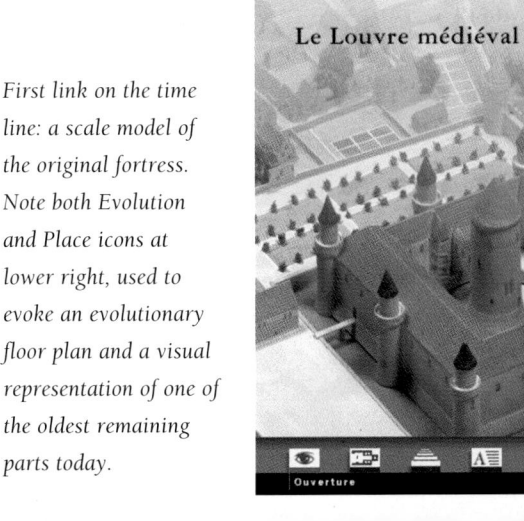

A Propos: the story of David and Bathsheba.

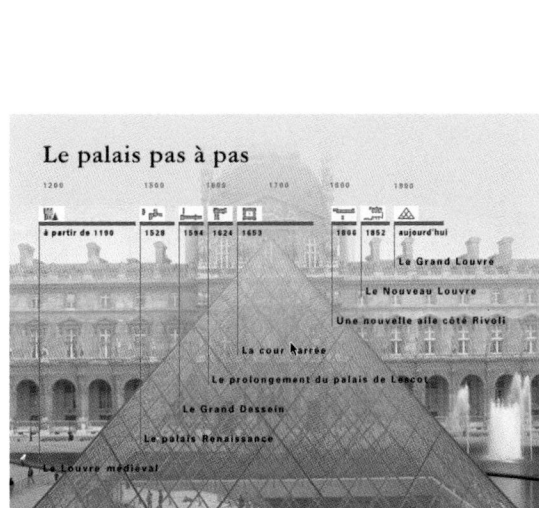
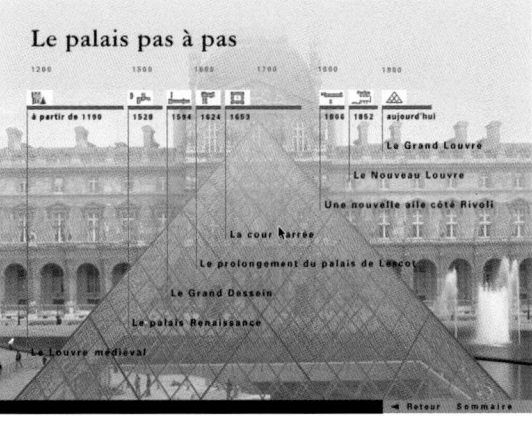

Eight centuries of the Louvre, step by step, with links arranged on time line.

First link on the time line: a scale model of the original fortress. Note both Evolution and Place icons at lower right, used to evoke an evolutionary floor plan and a visual representation of one of the oldest remaining parts today.

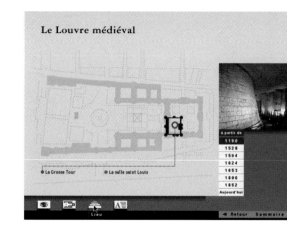

Le Louvre médiéval

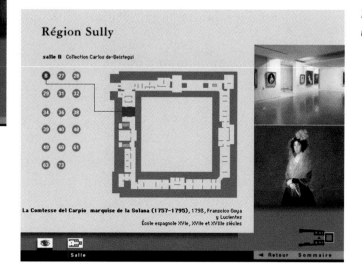

Région Sully

salle B Collection Carlos de-Beistegui

La Comtesse del Carpio marquise de la Solana (1757-1795), 1793, Franscico Goya y Lucientes
École espagnole XVIe, XVIIe et XVIIIe siècles

Screen activated by Evolution (floor plan) and Lieu (place) icons.

Région Sully of the Louvre, accessed by the links next to the main link on the main interface.

Région Sully

Exploring the Sully section and the biography of its namesake.

By concentrating on the information inherent in the visual qualities of the architecture and art of the Louvre, and limiting the amount of visual representation and commentary to an absolute minimum, the makers have succeeded in filtering out unnecessary complexity and yet creating a remarkably **comprehensive** survey. A better approach to this towering institution and all that it embraces can hardly be imagined.

JAMES BOEKBINDER

Pausing to look at one of the paintings it contains.

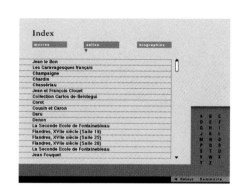

Index

The index

Sommaire

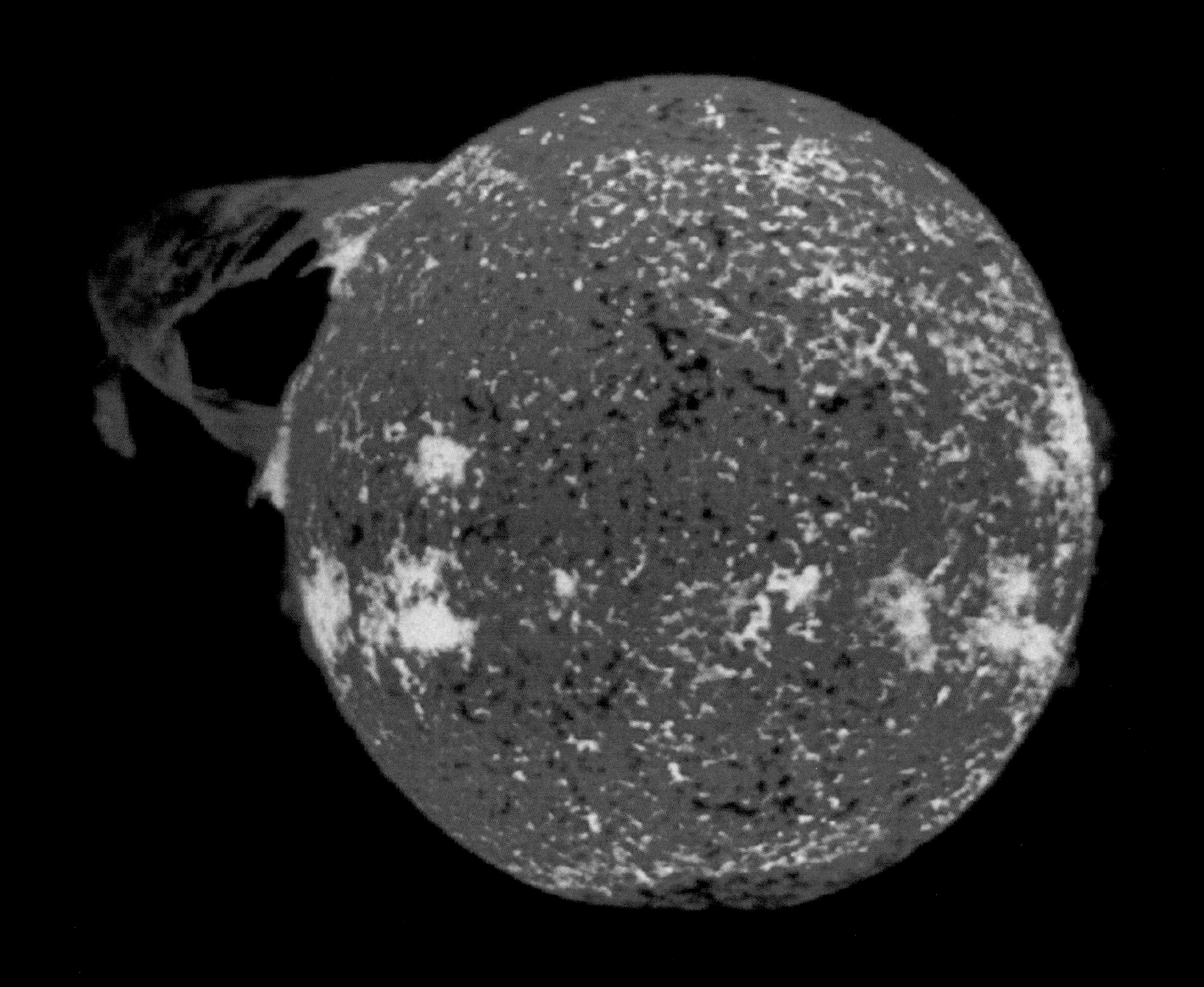

Redshift / Maris Multimedia Ltd.

You may get lost in outer space, but this easy–to–use view on Earth restores a sense of direction. Except perhaps for alien pilots.

Twenty–one thousand kilometres above the Earth. The pop up window at bottom left offers background information.

Pinpointing a location and clicking on it makes a information box appear that offers clear and precise information on its whereabouts.

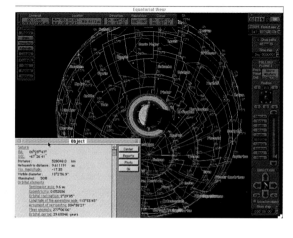

179

Redshift sets out to capture the galactic universe in one sole interactive disc and manages to do so in a very graceful and complete manner. The one dominating feature of **astronomy** is that it is not easily explained. It was the science of a few decades ago, when expansion into new territory meant outer space, and it had an aura of a higher science which only the potential or real–time rocket scientist would grasp. Redshift ends this; anyone with a sincere interest in space will experience dramatic and realistic views of space by using just a few simple controls.

For more data on a subject, various reports can be generated.

Clicking on the buttons, a chart is drawn up within seconds.

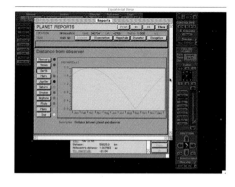

Year of publication 1993 **Author** Maris Multimedia Ltd. **Place of publication** London, UK **Publisher** Maris Multimedia Ltd. **Copyright owners** Maris Multimedia Ltd. **Awards** Information World Review: CD-ROM of the Year '95, Milia '94 Multimedia Awards: Jury's Special Prize, European Space Agency Technology Award '93, Parents Choice Gold Medal '94, BIMA Gold Award for Information '94, New Media Invision Gold Award for Adult Enrichment '94

Design company Maris Multimedia Ltd. **Screen design** Andre Zat, Anton Markov, Anton Lensk, Tatiana Cherno **Animation / graphics** Jacqueline Mitton, Tatiana Cherno **Production** Maris Multimedia Ltd., Nick Maris **Editors** Yuri Kolyuka **Platform** mac / mpc

All the possible data ever gathered by scientific stargazers has been brought together on Redshift. An easy to use direction panel makes travel through the abstract data extremely comfortable. View the Earth at the Julian date of 244491.4583, from the heliocentric distance of **1.016610** au at a Vis. magnitude of –22.51. Its all there; in a blink of an eye, the pulling down of a menu, within one screen, all the secrets of the universe are unfolded.

If Earth gets to be boring, the location can be changed by a click of the finger to Venus, choosing the view from the planet outwards, just one of six options. If you are wondering what the bright yellow spot in the velvet distance is, you will zoom in on the Sun, clickable by a pink **bull's eye** cursor. Another click will create a window volunteering information that the RA is 12h40m22s at a visible diameter of 44'2.7".

If and when an astronomical term is unknown to the user, the Penguin Dictionary of Astronomy is at hand.

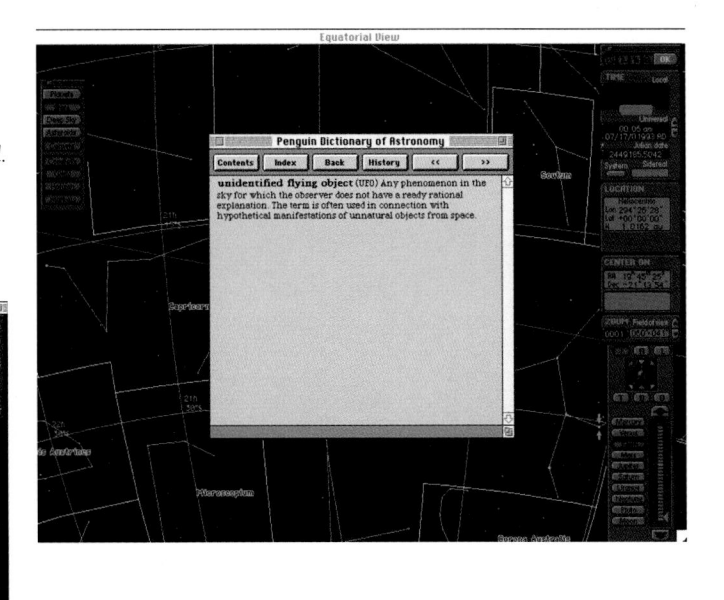

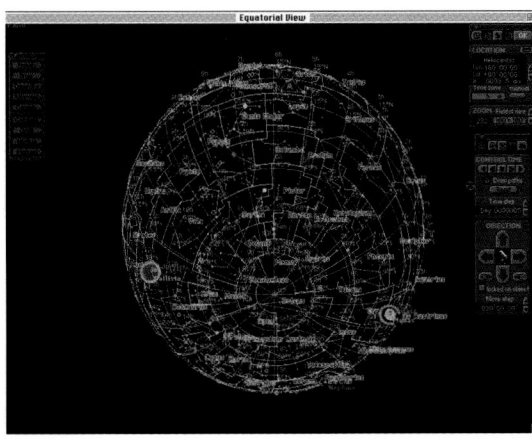

What started out as the location of the sun in the universe becomes a complete map of the universe when all available buttons are activated.

Floating around in space, looking at planet Earth...

...and looking up your zodiac sign from a somewhat greater distance.

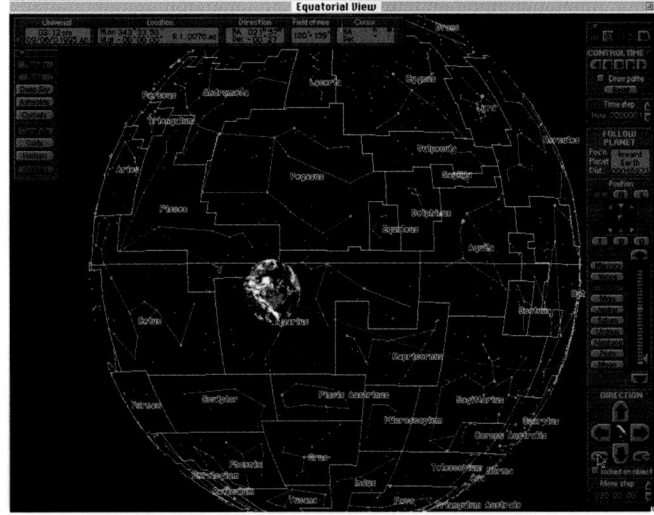

Make the earth spin, come closer, and be amazed.

Further inquisitiveness on this exploratory **voyage** through the space realm gives instant access to the extensive photo gallery, which, in a clear window, displays (mostly NASA) shots of the golden globe in a state of gargantuan prominence, for example. Hidden underneath the buttons is the Penguin Dictionary of Astronomy, with hypertext links making the CD–ROM into an endless plunge of infotainment.

Redshift captures centuries of scientific knowledge and presents it in the way the astronomer studies it: with **jumping digits** shown by robust meters, with time, space or elongation angles placed in colourful diagrams while the zoom power and location of the telescope are unequalled by any research institute or satellite in the waking world. Redshift has achieved a unique kind of space travel, using the digits of Read Only Memory.

ADAM EEUWENS

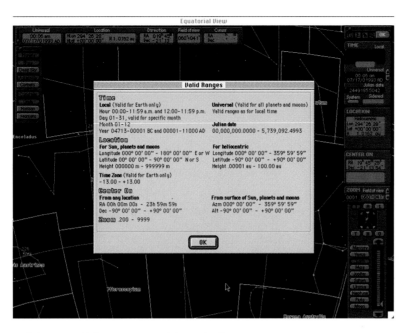

Valid ranges while staying overnight at Earth.

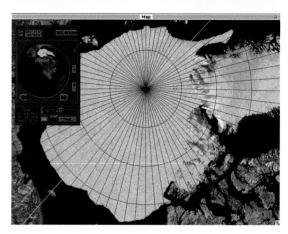

Discover the white top of our world.

Earth.

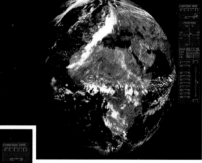

Take a look from the moon at a beautiful 'earthrise'.

addresses

Blender Magazine
Blender@sonicnet.com
Jenny von Feldt/Dennis International
25 West 39th St. #1103 NY, NY 10018, USA
tel: 212-302 2626
fax: 212-302 2635

ABCD Digizine
abcd@szocio.tgi.bme.hu
IDG Hungary - ABCD Studio
1012 Budapest, Márvány utca 17, Hungary
tel: 156-2967
fax: 156-9773

An Anecdoted Archive from the Cold War
legrady@mercury.sfsu.edu
George Legrady / Hyperreal Media Productions
bASE.ARTS, P.O. BOX 78154, San Francisco,
CA 94107, USA
tel: 415-821 4989
e-mail: base@well.sf.ca.us

ScruTiny in the Great Round
jimg@well.com
Calliope Media, 1526 Cloverfield Boulevard,
Santa Monica, California 90404-3502
SruTiny Associates: Jim Gasperini /
Tennessee Rice Dixon
270 Riverside Drive 12A, New York,
NY 10025, USA
tel: 212-666 6542

Une Promenade dans l'art du XX-eme siècle -
Foundation Marguerite et Aimé Maeght
Matra Hachette MultiMedia - Maeght Editeur
12, Rue Carvès, 92120 Montrouge, France
tel: 4746 8610
fax: 4746 0532

Registros de Arquitectura
Registros@pa.upc.es
Vicente Guallart (guallart@servicom.es)
Producciones New Media SL
Nou de la Rambla 24 pral,
08001 Barcelona, Spain
tel: 3-3180377
fax: 3-3020247

Le Louvre
Montparnasse Multimédia /
Réunion des Musées Nationaux
67, Rue de Richelieu, 75002 Paris
10, Impasse Robiquet, 75006 Paris, France
tel: 1-4548 1046
fax: 1-4548 9469

Puppet Motel
The Voyager Company
1 Bridge Street, Irvington, NY 10533, USA
tel: 914-591 5500
fax: 914-591 6484

She Loves it, She Loves it Not:
Women and Technology
Christine Tamblyn
835 Lenox Ave, Apt 212, Miami Beach,
FL 33139, USA
tel: 305-532 8841

Doors of Perception 1
desk@mediamatic.nl
Netherlands Design Institute
Mediamatic IP
Postbus 17490, 1001 JL Amsterdam, Netherlands
tel: 020-626 6262
fax: 020-626 3793

Commander Blood
Microfolie's Editions
Cryo Interactive Entertainment,
24, rue Marc Seguin; 75018 Paris, France
tel: 1-4465 2565
fax: 1-4607 7105

Bio•morph Encyclopedia Muybridge
4D. / Nobuhiro Shibayama
Kaori Murata
250 Mercer Street, suite c611
NY, NY 10012, USA
tel: 212-529 0599
fax: 212-995 2568

Echo Lake
hsherman@delrina.com
Delrina
895 Don Mills Road 500-2 Park Centre,
Toronto, Ontario M3C 1W3, Canada
tel: 416-466-8079
fax: 1-800-879-805

VOLVO Airbag
desk@mediamatic.nl
Paul Groot / Jans Possel
Mediamatic IP
Postbus 17490, 1001 JL Amsterdam, Netherlands
tel: 020-626 6262
fax: 020-626 3793

Pop Up Computer
ASK / TX / SOFTX
2-6 Shimomiyabi-cho, Shinjuku-ku,
Tokyo 162, Japan
tel: 03-3267 7341
fax: 03-3267 4471

Dragon Lore
Mindscape International Ltd.
Priority House, Charles Avenue, Maltings Park,
Burgess Hill, West Sussex, RH15 9PQ, UK
tel: 144-424 6333
fax: 144-424 8996
Cryo Interactive Entertainment
24, rue Marc Seguin; 75018 Paris, France.
tel: 1-4465 2565
fax: 1-4607 7105

Redshift
redshift@maris.com
Maris Multimedia Ltd.
99 Mansell Street, London E1 8AX
fax: (0)171-702-0534

ZeitMovie & Selected Notes 2 Zeitguys
aufwar@aol.com
Emigre & Zed
183 the Alameda, San Anselmo, CA 94960, USA
tel/fax: 415-721 7921

Pinch
bradj@bradjohnson.com
Brad Johnson
937 Grayson Street, Berkeley, CA 94710, USA
tel: 510-649 8444

POK le Petit Peintre
Arborescence
113, rue Anatole, Paris, France
92300 Levallois Perret, France
tel: 1-4757 3838
fax: 1-4757 3703

La Vague Interactive
Les Éditions Numériques
minitel: 3615 LVI
LVI-Presse
50-52, Rue Edouard Pailleron,
75019 Paris, France
tel: 1-4803 3117

Aux Origines de l'Homme
Microfolie's Editions
17, Avenue Duquesne, 75007 Paris, France
tel: 1-4551 4393
fax: 1-4551 4842

Magic Carpet
Bullfrog Productions
20 Nugent Road, Surrey Research Park, Guildford
GV2 5AF, UK
or via Electronic Arts; PO Box 835, Slough,
Berkshire, England SL3 8XU

UnZip
Zone (UK) Ltd.
8 Peartree Street, London EC1V 3SB, UK
tel: 171-250-3040
fax: 171-250-3925

The Digital City
http://www.dds.nl
De Digitale Stad
Kleine Gartmanplantsoen 10,
1017 RR, Amsterdam, Netherlands
tel: 020-6233673
fax: 020-6384489

HotWired
hot-info@hotwired.com
HotWired Ventures L.L.C.
520 3rd Street 4th Floor, San Francisco,
CA 94107, USA
tel: 415-222 6338
fax: 415-222 6369

Women at Risk for HIV
Carolyn Sherins
csherins@covina.lightside.com
Art Center College Of Design,
1772 Grevelia Street, South Pasadena,
CA 91030, USA
tel: 818-441 7743

House / Huis
Joost Grootens
J.M. Kemperstraat 107-I,1051 TM,
Amsterdam, Netherlands
tel/fax: 020-6886117

Improvisation Technologies
ZKM Karlsruhe / Ballet Frankfurt
ZKM, Gartenstrasse 71, 76135 Karlsruhe, BRD
tel: 721-9340 420
fax: 721-9340 429

Informer
Informer Interactive Research Ltd.
5 Sunbury House, Hocker St., Shoreditch,
London, E2 7LE, UK
Studio No 45. 33-35 St. John's Square, London
EC1M 4DS, UK
tel: 171-490-3043

P.A.W.S.
Domestic Funk Products
Little Shalwyn; Three Gates Lane; Hoslewere,
Surrey GU27 2LG, UK.
tel/fax: 1428 653 445
e-mail: dwf@gn.apc.org

Le Cri Néerlandais
The Netherlands Design Institute
Keizersgracht 609, 1017 DS, Amsterdam,
Netherlands
tel: 020-5516500
fax: 020-6201031

Bad Day on the Midway
inform@inscape.com
Inscape
1933 Pontius Avenue, Los Angeles,
CA 90025, USA
tel: 310-312 5705
fax: 310-312 6677

ISDM Website
Michael Samyn, Zupergraphyx!
Napoleon Annicqstraat 51, 9600 Ronse, Belgium
tel: 55-208863

StarDOTstar Shopping Mall
www.xs4all.nl/~sculptro/index.htm
Lars Eijssen
Sarphatistraat 410, 1018 GW,
Amsterdam, Netherlands
tel/fax: 020-6205722

The Way Things Work
Dorling Kindersley Multimedia
9 Henrietta Street, London WCZE 8PS, UK
tel: 0171-836 5411
fax: 0171-379 0057

Call for entries

multimedia graphics 2

Multimedia Graphics is the international sourcebook of the world's best multimedia productions.

The projects showcased in this book have been selected from a huge array of recent work. For the second edition of Multimedia Graphics you can submit new work. For entry form contact:

BIS Publishers

Nieuwe Spiegelstraat 36

1017 DG Amsterdam

The Netherlands

Phone: + (0)20 6205 171

Fax : + (0)20 6279 251

Email: bispub@xs4all.nl

colophon

Editors

Mediamatic, Amsterdam
Willem Velthoven, Amsterdam, willem@mediamatic.nl
Jorinde Seijdel, Amsterdam, jorinde@xs4all.nl

Editorial production

Mediamatic, Amsterdam
Guido Schrijvers, Amsterdam
Jorinde Seijdel, Amsterdam

Corresponding editors

Florian Brody, Vienna, brody@newmedia.co.at
Melissa Dallal, New York City, mdallal@panix.com
Véronique Godé & Maxence Layet, Paris
Jacinta Hin & Yutaka Yano, Tokyo, jacinta@twics.com
Rafael Lozano-Hemmer, Madrid, 75337.1453@compuserve.com
Giles Rollestone, London, g.rollestone@rca.ac.uk
Meral Yasar, Budapest, meral@szocio.tgi.bme.hu

Authors

Neville Brody, London, ag62@mailhost.cityscape.co.uk
Florian Brody, Vienna, brody@newmedia.co.at
Greg Ball, Enschede
James Boekbinder, Amsterdam, boekbind@xs4all.nl
Max Bruinsma, Amsterdam, maxb@xs4all.nl
Melissa Dallal, New York City, mdallal@panix.com
Ben de Dood, Amsterdam, bendd@mail.euronet.nl
Adam Eeuwens, Amsterdam, flux@wave.riv.nl
Jules Marshall, Amsterdam, jules@xs4all.nl
Geert J. Strengholt, Amsterdam, geertjan@mediamatic.nl
Willem Velthoven, Amsterdam, willem@mediamatic.nl

Design

Rick Vermeulen and Tjø van Zuijlen, Inízio, Amsterdam